THE
UNDERDOGS

CONQUERING LIFE WITH
MAN'S BEST FRIEND AND SEAL TEAM ▮

CHIEF PETTY OFFICER
BENITO OLSON, USN (RET.)
WITH DARREN SAPP

Ballast Books, LLC
www.ballastbooks.com

ISBN: 978-1-962202-03-9

Printed in Hong Kong

Published by Ballast Books
www.ballastbooks.com

For more information, bulk orders, appearances, or speaking requests, please email: info@ballastbooks.com

This book is dedicated to my wife, Erica, and my children, Jacob and Emma. Without them, I honestly don't know where I'd be. I've seen dark times, and because of my family, I have been able to persevere. They have been there for me and for each other while I have gone out into the world serving in the U.S. Navy. I've always said I'm doing this for them, and I think that's what has been able to save me.

CONTENTS

" It never troubles the wolf how many the sheep may be.

—Virgil

EDDIE PENNEY

T he Navy SEAL community is a small, tight-knit group that rarely allows outside influences to penetrate its sacredness. As you move to the more selective units, things get exponentially more sacred. Those of us fortunate enough to rise to that level protect its culture as if it were an endangered species.

We weren't into outsiders. The nature of our operations, though, dictated that our teams needed outside support to complete the mission. We worked with explosive ordnance disposal (EOD) specialists, dog handlers, tactical air controllers, and pararescuemen on nearly every mission. That being said, only true, reliable *assets* are permitted to work alongside SEAL assaulters. There is no exception to this. You either help the mission, or you get sent packing. The operator lifestyle demands that you face and inflict death nightly; there's no room for dead weight.

I first met Benny somewhere in the whirlwind training/alert/deployment cycle while serving as a breacher and assaulter at the Navy SEALs ████. I was a seasoned combat operator with over a decade of military service in the SEAL teams at the time. Benny was the dog handler attached to our assault troop working up and training for our next deployment to Iraq. He was a master-at-arms (MA), not a SEAL. He was going to have to prove his worth to the team. I was one of those guilty men who wondered to myself: *Is he good enough to be here? Is he going to be an asset or a liability to me, my brothers, and the mission?*

Benny quickly put my hesitation to rest. He listened, watched, learned, adapted, and quickly became a great asset to our mission from the way that he ran his dog to accomplish any tasks that were his responsibility. He pulled his weight and then some. You could see that he was a sponge and soaked up all knowledge that was thrown his way. He wasn't just a taker in the wisdom department but also a giver. He taught us how we could work more effectively around the dog while on target, especially when the dog was tracking or attacking a target (which was the best part, by the way).

Op after op, night after night of taking the fight to the enemy, Benny proved his place within our team. He was not a talker but a doer. His mindset was straight and pointing true north on destroying the terror that surrounded us. Through his humility, he will always tell you he is "just a dog guy," but the fact is that he is an awesome operator who always got the job done. More importantly, he is a good human being. Minus his love for the Minnesota Vikings, he is a humble and caring man.

When working in the environments that we did, the risk of injury was constant. The job we were doing was real—real enough that people would die and get maimed. For Benny, this risk became a harsh reality. We were on an op together in Iraq, chasing a terror network that liked to use suicide vests and house-borne improvised explosive devices (HBIEDS). IEDs presented a great threat to us and were widely used since they were mostly homemade. Just a week earlier, we witnessed one of these terrorists blow himself and children up just so he would not have to face our team. He knew his time was up, so he took his family with him. These guys were hardcore terrorists.

As I describe in my own book, *UNAFRAID*, our assaulters were stacked on the target building, preparing to make entry, when an HBIED went off, collapsing the entire structure. One of our assaulters was killed, and several others, including Benny, were wounded. He sustained a double femur compound fracture that would send him home for recovery. I can remember pulling off the debris and rubble that covered his wounded body and carrying him to our Bradley fighting vehicles for exfil. Seeing the extreme pain on his face left a lasting impression on my soul. Though Benny sustained such a serious injury, he did what not many would do. He bounced back and put the operator gear back on. Benny's mindset had a different plan. He inspired us all and is a true warrior.

Benny shared with me that he was writing this book and asked if I would write his foreword. I was beyond honored to be asked. He has made a lasting impression on me that I have carried through as a father, as a husband, and as a man who wants to be the best I can be. His mindset is simple. Make it work—get it done! Life will throw obstacles, but the correct mindset will destroy all!

EDDIE PENNEY, Texas, USA

Eddie retired after twenty years of military service. He owns and operates Contingent Group, a global risk mitigation service. He is also the creator of the UNAFRAID brand, a warrior mindset speaker, and the author of *UNAFRAID: Staring Down Terror as a Navy SEAL and Single Dad.*

AUTHOR'S NOTE

When I decided to write this book, my intent was to share my story with as many people as I could. I wanted to be heard. What I didn't realize was that I could help someone else who has gone through, or is currently going through, similar situations. Too many times in life, we find ourselves as the underdog. Throughout my life, I don't think others considered me to be the favorite to come out on top or to be the victor, yet here I am! This book is simply about that.

I know about being an underdog. I grew up with an alcoholic stepfather (my real father went to prison) and endured countless other challenges that could have broken me, but I chose to use them to get stronger. I overcame some stiff odds and wound up killing it. I served at the highest levels of the United States military, eventually operating with SEAL Team ██. I didn't give a damn what anyone said about my ability to succeed; I just did succeed through stubbornness and not knowing how to fail.

Secret squirrel shit I'm not supposed to talk about

Let me clarify before you read any more—I wasn't a SEAL, was never a SEAL, and have never claimed to be a SEAL. That distinction is important because as many times as I've reiterated that fact, people continue to mistakenly refer to me as a SEAL. I was fortunate enough for the U.S. Navy to attach me to that elite special operations group, and I served in combat alongside them—as well as my dogs.

But I chose a slightly different path. I believe, in some respects, I was cut from the same cloth as those guys. I have the same personality and mentality, but I didn't have the desire to become a SEAL. First of all, if you ever saw me swim, you would quickly realize I'm more rock than fish. I'm not sure why, but it's probably because I skipped swim class, afraid of the girls seeing my junk through my shorts. I can float. I can run. But I can only swim enough to save my life. Aside from that, I hate to swim. Still, I joined the military's aquatic branch, so make of that what you will.

I have led an interesting life's journey and not what you might call typical. This is more evident than ever when examining my military career. I joined the National Guard, then quit the National Guard, joined the U.S. Navy, became a dog handler, went to SEAL Team ██, lost brothers that I never knew I would have prior to joining, experienced post-traumatic stress disorder (PTSD), became addicted to opioids, contemplated suicide, left the service, and started a business working with dogs and training their owners. Now, I'm in the movies—well, at least the dogs are.

You're going to read some messed-up shit within these pages, but that messed-up shit is what made me the man I am today. I'm not perfect, but I'm still here when there are plenty of reasons why I shouldn't be. I call that a win, and within these pages, I believe you'll find a win for yourself. Do you feel like an underdog? If you do, I hope my story inspires you to rise above, disprove the haters, and overcome that little voice that says you can't do something—because you can. I did, and you can too.

———

About the redactions, the solid, black-colored blocking of certain words or phrases: I'm honored to have served on the best SEAL team in the US arsenal. The Department of Defense reviewed this manuscript and dictated certain information they did not want me to share about that team. I chose to make some adjustments but left many redactions, trusting the reader to infer the missing words in the context they're presented.

CHAPTER 1
HELLCHILD

So there I lay, covered in a fucking building. Not as in "the enemy had our building covered" or "we took cover in a building." As in a building had crumbled on top of me. A house, actually, or what remained of one. It was like hundreds of others in that ancient land of Iraq. This particular building had been obliterated by a terrorist we had been searching for prior to the detonation.

I remember that night vividly. February 7, 2008, in Baqubah—a particularly violent Iraqi city of about half a million, thirty miles northeast of Baghdad. The U.S. Navy had attached me, along with my dog, Digo, a sixty-five-pound lunatic hellchild Belgian Malinois, with a troop of SEALs. Digo definitely had a few screws loose but also had the tenacity of a pit bull, the loyalty of a retriever, the smarts of a show poodle, and the hunting instincts of a wolf. And he was all mine.

We had rolled out of Forward Operating Base Warhorse in the dead of the night and loaded into big, eight-wheeled armored fighting vehicles called Strykers, ready to kick some terrorist ass. I can't get into exact numbers or details for operational security, but I can say that a SEAL troop consisted of four elements—three assault teams and one sniper team. Then, there was me and Digo, plus a number of other direct support personnel.

On the way in, I always had music from my iPod Nano going in one ear and comms going in the other. I'm a Christian, but I will say that, back then, my choice of music wasn't entirely godly. Then again, I'm not sure how pumped I could be listening to worship music when I knew damn well what I was about to go do. The song I chose to play on repeat was "The Beautiful People"—only because of the beat. I had no idea who Marilyn Manson was. Was it my most shining moment? No, but the song did get me locked in.

Digo and I had the job of working up front with the SEAL snipers during the patrol so that the dog could sniff out any IEDs or hidden enemy fighters along the route. Then, once on target (at the target of the mission), we'd rotate between the three assault teams, designated Alpha, Bravo, and Kilo, remaining with whoever was assigned as the main assault force. Digo and I always wanted to work with the main assault team, and that's where they wanted us, the dog up front and ready to root out the bad guys.

Typically, I'd want the dog twenty to thirty yards in front of the patrol in order to make sure that, if anything like an IED or hidden combatants looking to do us harm popped up, we'd have enough distance between us and harm's way. That always made me a bit nervous because if I looked away for a couple of seconds, my dog would be off running, and then I'd have to locate him. I'm not saying I would lose my dog, but after glancing away for a brief moment while wearing a night optical/observation device (NODs), trying to find something that's moving becomes difficult. I did have an easy way to locate him, however.

That particular night's mission called for us to capture or kill an Al-Qaeda in Iraq (AQI) terrorist financier. It came three days after a cat-astrophic mission not far from that compound in a small village on the outskirts of the city where we had lost two amazing operators.

As we neared the target location, we dismounted and continued the rest of the way on foot. Maintaining as much stealth as possible, we slowly crept to the target building. We certainly didn't want to wake up the city, so we knocked out any operable streetlights, ensuring we'd stay in the dark and, hopefully, undetected. Darkness always gave us the advantage because we had night vision capabilities, and the bad guys didn't. Plus, Digo didn't need to see to find bad guys—that's what his nose was for.

Due to the United States' hasty exit from Afghanistan, I pray we never have to go back there because we handed over so many night vision goggles (NVGs) to the Afghan Army that we wouldn't have this advantage now. We screwed ourselves royally by providing such capabilities to an Afghan Army that's not prepared to take control of their country. We might as well have just given the equipment to the Taliban. Would they maintain the equipment for future use? Probably not, but the fact that they have it drives me nuts.

I carried a heavy complement of gear and weapons as well as my partner on a three-foot lead. So there I was on a cool, winter night in Baqubah, Iraq, standing outside a terrorist compound with my killer dog and a bunch of the baddest warriors this nation has ever produced. Little did I know that my wife would give birth to my son just three weeks later, and he was about to come damn close to growing up without a father.

Ready for anything, we closed in on the building where our target hid, and our team set up a perimeter. Then, our interpreter pulled out his bullhorn to tell everyone inside to come out. We knew the enemy liked to rig houses to blow, so we wanted to avoid rushing in if we could help it. Besides, that's why we brought the dogs. The last thing we wanted was for a dog to get hurt or injured breaching a target—actually, that's the second-to-last thing we wanted to happen. This may sound callous, but while I loved my dogs, if someone had to go home draped in an American flag, I'd rather it be the dog than one of the boys. So we always sent a dog in first to sniff out any barricaded fighters or suicide bombers.

This was my first deployment, and no amount of training could prepare me for a real firefight. So far, everything had gone smoothly, and no one had fired any rounds. I looked down at Digo. I could tell, like always, he seemed eager to go in and take care of business—chomping at the bit, one could say. I watched as he homed in on every Iraqi that exited the building. A woman and child came out first. Then, one after another, the house's occupants exited peaceably, though that didn't stop Digo from wanting to steal an easy bite. Most of the dogs we worked with, at least the good ones, were always looking for an opportunity to get a free bite. Some, a little too much. In fact, that's how I'd inherited Digo. Another SEAL Team ▮ squadron had kicked him off their team for getting in a few too many free bites on the good guys. That's where I knew I had to be smarter than the beast—easier said than done since those dogs are so intelligent. I always kept my head on a swivel to ensure Digo never got a free bite on any of the people under our control.

Accidental bites were a sure way of getting your ass investigated, and I wanted no part of that. If I couldn't control Digo, they'd send him home, and I'd have no dog. Without a dog, I wouldn't be on deployment, and if I wasn't on deployment, I wouldn't have the honor to remain out there on target with those operators. And that's where I wanted to be. I legitimately felt that with Digo at my side, we were unstoppable—to a point, it seemed.

As the last few people exited the target house, gunfire started popping off. Suddenly, the pending conflict became clear and present. Two men tried to exit the building holding AK-47s. The SEALs providing overwatch promptly dropped them in the doorway. After a few tense moments, two more people came out, unarmed, stepping over the bodies. We waited, trying to determine whether anyone remained in the house. I knew there was a good chance our team leader would soon call out, "Dog up," and we'd send in Digo to find out.

I began thinking how best to get him into the house. I wanted to avoid the door if I could. Bad guys expected us to use the door. I peered around the corner and saw a big bay window. Perfect. I could chuck Digo in that way, allowing him to surprise anyone inside who didn't want to play by the rules. No one would expect a fur missile to explode through the window. I always looked for the next advantage or spot where the dog could be most useful.

As the moment approached, I remained convinced that the window gave us the best opportunity. While it wasn't our turn yet, I would make sure Digo stayed ready.

Finally, after everyone exited, we sent the last female back in to open all the curtains and sheets covering the doorways. We told her to make sure everyone had come out because we would release Digo—and Digo did not discriminate. He would spare no one given the opportunity—men, women, kids, grandparents, etc. When we told Digo to bite, he'd bite. Did I want him to bite unarmed people? Of course not. That's why we gave them all the chances in the world to come out the easy way. We were sent on these missions for the bad guys, and we wanted any innocents to step out of the way. But that was war, and war ain't pretty.

When the girl returned, she informed our interpreter that one man refused to come out. She said he had only arrived a few days previously. Bingo. We now knew we had our guy. After hearing that, I became even more excited, adrenaline pumping through me like a broken pipe, though I'm sure the Rip It energy drink I'd chugged before leaving the base contributed.

Our interpreter got on the bullhorn again to announce that we were sending in the dogs, and the SEAL leader told me to make Digo bark. No problem. I looked down and spoke to him in Dutch: "*Gib Laut.*" A command for him to speak.

Digo promptly went berserk. Frantic, hyper barks penetrated the air, echoing against the buildings like a demon's call. At that point, he was lit. If that guy heard Digo and still didn't want to give up, he probably had a death wish.

I reached down and grabbed Digo's vest. "*Braaf,*" I said—"good dog" in Dutch.

We waited. No one came out.

The call, "Dog up," came through my earpiece.

No more chances. Go time.

I then called over the radio, "Dog up," to let the team leader know I was ready.

He replied, "Send it."

I knelt down next to Digo and felt his tense body radiating energy through my grip on his tactical vest. With no need for stealth, I had to let him embrace his animal instincts and show his love for his job. Froth flew from his mouth as he barked like a dog possessed.

"*Stellen*," I commanded, releasing his vest and slapping him on the ass. That instructed him to bite, and Digo fucking sent it. There was no chill with this dog. Just full send. Like the fur missile he was, he exploded into the courtyard, sprinting toward the dropped terrorists sprawled in the doorway. Dead meat. His favorite. Digo loved to hit dead prey. It was like a free reward for him.

He began tearing at the bodies, latching on and tugging at them. Due to their literal dead weight, he couldn't budge them far, but he sure tried. One thing was for certain: Neither was playing possum. It wasn't pretty but was a good use for the dog. The bad guys would sometimes fake death to suck a person in and then set off their suicide vests or grenades. I never wanted to walk over somebody unsure of their status, so I'd absolutely send the dog. I would never do that if the target had already been confirmed secured, but if the target wasn't secure, it absolutely did help the dog and let the team know that the dog would engage.

However, I now needed Digo to leave the eliminated threats alone and get into the house to find the current one. As much as I tried to push him past the dead bodies, he just kept going back to get mouthfuls of free play. Finally, I recalled Digo to me at the compound entrance and told my team leader that we weren't going through the doorway. I needed to get a tad closer to get Digo in. I had already identified the perfect method.

"That bay window," I said.

"Roger that," the team leader replied.

Our team moved inside the compound. Once in the courtyard, we felt incredibly exposed because we couldn't hug the walls for protection. We had about twenty feet or so between the wall and the house, so getting to the actual building for cover definitely drove my preference for the bay window. That also allowed me to avoid navigating around the three or four other bodies at the carport. After I bypassed the bodies and the door, my focus shifted to that bay window. Digo, another assaulter, and I crept over to it while the team leader gave the plan over comms.

"I'm going to put a frag through the doorway. Then, send the dog," he instructed.

Check. My team leader, due to the potential threat inside, wanted to soften up any barricaded shooters with a grenade and give Digo a better chance. As I said, it's better that the dog eat a bullet instead of one of us, but we never wanted to send the dog in on a suicide mission.

I replied that Digo was ready and that I was going to send him through the window.

Just before they tossed the frag, I got on both knees and ducked below the bay window, clutching Digo so we wouldn't eat shit from the grenade's explosion.

"Frag out, frag out," came through comms.

After it went off, I rose and looked into the window to shove Digo through it. In that short moment, it seemed like so much time passed or that time was frozen. Suddenly, I felt an incredible pressure coming back in my face. It felt like the strongest, most overbearing wind I'd ever encountered, and I knew something had gone wrong. I'd never experienced anything like it before. It lasted only for a split second, and then blackness overwhelmed me. I was out.

Suddenly, I came to. It seemed like I had been out a while, and I couldn't move anything. I couldn't feel anything. Everything remained black. I felt like I was stuck. Buried.

What the fuck just happened? And where's Digo? My teammates? Are they okay? Did they forget about me? Was I buried alive in my grave? I had no clue what had just happened.

I didn't know it at the time, but that initiated the most difficult test of my life, both mentally and physically. It would take everything I had in me to come back.

CHAPTER 2
THE MAKING OF AN UNDERDOG

How did a kid from South St. Paul, Minnesota, wind up running missions with the SEAL teams? Both fate and grit played their parts, as you'll see as I share my ethos for overcoming situations when life painted me as an underdog.

I'll state this again clearly so there's no misunderstanding: I'm not a U.S. Navy SEAL. I do, however, understand the confusion. I served, step for step, on deployment, on missions, with the SEAL teams. We would infil on the same helicopters, shoot the same bad guys, and assault the same buildings. If I sound sensitive, it's because I am. Stolen valor exists, and when you're a guy trying to share your story that's entwined with that of a unit known the world over, it's important to make sure there's no misunderstanding.

While I wasn't a SEAL, I helped them do their job. Bottom line, they couldn't do some of the stuff they did without guys like me (and the dogs) doing what we did. That's not me being arrogant but rather me sharing that there are so many moving parts of the machine that make the mission successful. SEALs are great at executing the objective, but when they don't want to handle dogs, comms, etc., and there are guys like me who are willing to step in—although some SEALs did see the benefits to becoming a dog handler and pursued that path.

We handlers and our dogs are always right there in the action. We're the first thing the SEALs think of when spotting a squirter (an enemy who is running away), a barricaded shooter, or vehicle interdictions. For example, Will Chesney, a former SEAL Team █ operator, worked as the handler for Cairo, the most famous military working dog in history. "Cheese," as most call Will, and Cairo conducted the mission that killed Bin Laden. Doesn't get any cooler than that.

I enlisted in the U.S. Navy as an MA (military police officer) in 2003 and served all over the world, from Kingsville, Texas, to Bahrain to Iraq and Afghanistan. I was eventually selected to operate with the SEAL teams—a non-SEAL getting to do all the badass shit those elite warriors train years to do. I never thought I would be kicking in doors with those guys. I don't think I even knew that much about Navy SEALs growing up. Admittedly, when they selected me, I really didn't know the scope of what they'd have me doing. They didn't share much information other than basics, such as physical fitness, maturity, and a willingness to do some crazy-ass shit. I checked all those boxes.

But other than that, luck played a major factor, along with my attitude for seizing any opportunity placed in my path. Normally, I would say I'm not the type of person who would jump into something without knowing exactly what I was getting into because I'd consider that a recipe for disaster. But I now sometimes tell myself to just say yes and find out the more intricate details later because of my past experience. I never would have had that opportunity had I not just jumped in and said yes.

Never underestimate what God has in store for your life. You don't need to have everything figured out. I certainly didn't. And you don't need other people to hand you anything in order to get what you want out of life. Just because one door closes doesn't mean there isn't another one ready, wide open for you to step through. What you need is to believe in yourself. You need no one else's approval. What others think doesn't matter. What matters is having a fire burning inside that motivates you to do better—to recognize that when one door closes, you have to kick in the next door. Or the bay window, which, by the way, kicked my ass, but as it happens, that's life. No matter what, never stop. Never give up.

Even though I grew up in a small town, I always felt like I was meant to do something big with my life, even as a kid. Nothing screamed join the military or start my own business. However, something inside me yearned for more, like a constant fire. Nothing could extinguish it. At the same time, part of me felt like I was destined to work at the post office, at the packing house where they slaughtered cows, or even at 3M where my grandpa worked for so many years. I don't consider anything wrong with that, by the way. Typically, you are a product of your upbringing and will follow in the footsteps of your relatives. I simply did not.

As I look back at my childhood, I can't help but contemplate what an odd path I took. Even in high school, nothing suggested I would steer toward elite military service or entrepreneurship. I don't really remember having a career or education counselor who made it a point to talk to the students. However, most of the teachers and administrators generally pushed for us to go to college and get an education. They always taught the importance of making money, and to make the money, we had to go to school. Outside of that, I had no one pushing me to achieve a higher education. Hell, I didn't decide to go to a community college until the end of twelfth grade.

Had those counselors educated me on the opportunities open to me after high school, I would probably have chosen a different path. So in a sense, I'm happy that I didn't gain that knowledge, which would have put me on a different road—one that would have allowed me to have a solid livelihood but that would have limited my ability to accomplish all that I have ultimately achieved.

Nonetheless, I also have taken that information and am now raising my kids much differently. Imagine if high schools didn't tell kids they had to go to college to be successful. What if, instead, they taught kids that they could save thousands in tuition and start a business doing something that made them happy, as long as they had a vision and were prepared to work for it? That's what I'm teaching my children.

If not for that fire inside my soul, I would have been destined for a completely different path—one that didn't allow me to reach my fullest potential. I wasn't going to let my circumstances dictate my worth and sell myself short. When faced with adversity, we don't have to take "no" for an answer; we can chart our own course if we really want something.

The little town of South St. Paul was made famous by its stockyards, which existed for over 122 years. That world-leading center for livestock employed thousands, but in the span of a couple of decades, it essentially ceased to exist. We all used to hear the complaints about the smell that came from the stockyards, but now, looking back, that was South St. Paul—our way of life, however rough around the edges. It fueled the city and defined its inhabitants. But times, as they always do, changed. Meatpacking became more decentralized, and the market shifted. One by one, the stockyards closed down. Hundreds of blue-collar jobs vanished, just like that.

We needed those types of jobs, and my mom had one of them. She also worked at a candy store and gave her blood to feed us. I don't mean that figuratively. She would literally donate blood for money. I remember the permanent hole marks that I could see in my mom's arms from getting poked with a needle so frequently. They weren't a hallmark of drug use; they were a symbol of her constant trips to the clinic to give blood to feed her children. I simply can't imagine what my mom experienced at that time. It's because of her I don't have to do things like that.

I remember my mom waking up at the ass crack of dawn to go to work. She would take us over to our grandma and grandpa's house, and I wouldn't see her again until dark. As a child, the actual clock on the wall meant nothing to me because I knew I wouldn't see my mom until after the sun had set. While my grandparents did a wonderful job taking care of us, barely spending time with my mother took a toll on me. Never mind the fact that I had no father figure except weekends here or there whenever it was convenient for my parents to get along. But I understood why my mom had to be gone all day. That wasn't her fault—it was just the reality of it. She loved us very much and had to do what she had to do.

Until my mother met my stepdad, she lived the life of a single mom. It was all her. Was she perfect? In my eyes, yes. She was my mom. She did whatever she could to make sure my sister and I had clothes, food, and a roof over our heads.

My mom lived a very hard life, and I always found pride in how hard she worked through those struggles. It's really her example that defined my work ethic. I believe that experience of spending little time with my mother actually helped me leave home for the U.S. Navy and be away from everything I knew. It's never easy leaving your family for deployment, but when I needed to go, I didn't skip a beat. I understood what it meant to go away because I had to.

As a kid, I loved to play soccer, and I also played hockey at a local park in the winter. The city would come with water trucks and spray water, leaving us with an ice oasis. We couldn't afford for me to play real hockey in a league. Plus, the time commitment would have burdened my mom, who always worked. I know this now being a father to my daughter who is involved in travel hockey. So even though I couldn't play in a league and pursue a future career in the NHL like every kid I played with dreamed of, my cousin Brandon and I would grab our skates and hockey sticks and go down to Spruce Park. After school, on the weekends, really anytime we could, we went. These were probably some of the most fun times of my childhood. My old-school grandma made it easier because she'd simply kick us outside to play. We've all heard those phrases, "Go play" and "Don't come in until it's suppertime." She'd say things like that or threaten us with the dreaded "nap."

I loved playing my favorite hockey position at the park—goalie. I always viewed the goalie as the cornerstone of the team. I mean, really, if they played like shit and let in a ton of goals, the team would feel deflated and think they'd never catch up. However, if the goalie played lights out, then shit, the rest of the team could attack and keep attacking.

Whenever I think back to my childhood, playing hockey in Spruce Park always puts a smile on my face. Of course, it wasn't all smooth sailing. From time to time, other kids would try to take over the game, which inevitably resulted in fights. I know—shocking, right? Fighting in hockey. I may have lost some of those fights, but I always stood my ground. No one pushed me around. I was scrappy. Are there times I should have walked away? Absolutely, but even at a young age, I just felt like I had something to prove. So brave, so proud, and if I'm being honest, so stupid.

Regardless of how many fights I got into as a kid, I have always been a tenderhearted person. My wife tells me that all the time. Tough on the outside but sensitive as fuck on the inside and always drawn to some type of service.

As a kid in elementary school, I would volunteer to serve as a crossing guard. I would carry this damn flag for several streets, blocking traffic all the way. And because my grandma's house was all the way down on 7th Avenue, I was the last crossing guard. I'd wait until the last kid that I could see had crossed the street, and then I'd get to school after everyone else. I didn't mind it though because I always felt good about helping out. Young children relied on us to make sure traffic stopped so they could get to school safely. That volunteer work served as a precursor to joining the navy for sure.

We lived in a few places during my childhood until ultimately settling down on 8th Avenue in South St. Paul. However, I found living in the Woodmere Apartments over in Woodbury, Minnesota, the most memorable. I made lots of friends there, and we were always hanging out or riding bikes in the complex. We had this little pond where we'd pull out crawfish to play with. We'd never do anything mean to them, but we'd always get out there early to find the biggest one.

One day, I received one of those double-dog dares to take my plastic kid pool and cross the pond in it like George Washington crossing the Delaware. Looking back on it now, it's hard to fathom the stupid things I did because I could barely doggy paddle. Heck, even in the military, I had to learn how to actually move my arms and swim. I hated swim class in school. One, because it's always awkward learning in a coed swim class. Second, I wasn't a great swimmer. I swam well enough to not drown. Looking back on it, I wasn't even a great swimmer when I went to the SEAL teams. I barely passed that portion of the test. For that double-dog dare, I didn't know how deep the water was, but I refused to turn down a direct challenge, so I did it. When I got to the middle of the pond, my makeshift boat started taking on water. Scared shitless, I continued to the other side. I could see but a few inches deep in that murky water, and as a kid, my imagination ran wild as to what creatures lurked in the depths.

What can I say? We were boys. Being reckless and taking risks described that boyhood. Now, I know that the wonderful thing called social media and politically correct culture will say "boys will be boys" with a negative connotation. It's not that cut-and-dry. When boys were taught to respect girls and treat others with kindness, then boys being boys turned out just fine. I did a lot of stupid crap as a boy, and fuck, I'm happy because it allowed me to simply grow up and be whomever the hell I wanted to be. I didn't have people at school, trolls on the internet, or some other random assholes telling me that I needed to live a certain way or pushing me in a certain direction. My mother allowed me to chart my own path, and I'm damn proud of where it's taken me. I honestly wish society would just let kids be kids. So screw social media, and let boys be boys. Teach them to have respect and allow them to just be a boy.

I remember my son, Jacob, being told in kindergarten that he was not able to continue on to first grade because he was quiet and couldn't sit still. We decided to quickly pull him out of that school, and I mean it when I say do what you believe is correct. Not all educators are created equal. A year later, a lady by the name of Ms. Tracy got ahold of Jacob, and it was life changing. I remember her crying the day we left for Texas because she said it's because of kids like my son—kids who are written off because they don't fall into some category—that she does what she does. I learned early on that I needed to be my kids' advocate so he could chart his own path as I had been able to do.

When I was about eight years old, my mom dated this loser of a guy, and she ultimately ended it with him. Well, he didn't like that so much, and in the middle of the night, he chucked one of our toys through the sliding window of our apartment patio. That terrified me and seared into my head that no one should be made to feel afraid like that. The police came, and we had to spend the night at our friend's apartment. I didn't want to live a life of fear. I wanted to learn to take action when necessary.

As it happened, I had my first introduction to the military in that apartment. *Operation Desert Storm*, the liberation of Kuwait, and the battle with Saddam Hussein's Iraqi forces appeared on nearly every TV channel. My mom considered that a scary event, not knowing the type of outcome we'd see. As a kid, I didn't know what that meant, but I liked what I saw in those badasses dressed in military gear going off to do cool shit. Of course, after joining the military, I came to realize that 90 percent of the time is spent sitting and waiting while only 10 percent is filled with action. Nevertheless, that stuff looked cool, and I wanted to be part of it. That served as the inspiration for the future I was heading toward.

CHAPTER 3
FINDING GRIT

———————

I named this book *The Underdogs* in part because, at some point in life, we are all underdogs. Tom Brady, who has one of the biggest underdog stories of all, was selected 199th overall in the sixth round of the NFL draft. He certainly fits in that category. I already have and will continue to talk about why I've always been the underdog.

For example, I grew up with a stepdad who, for the most part, was okay. But did he make some mistakes? Absolutely. He was far from perfect.

Right before Christmas, when I was sixteen or so, the police surprised us with a knock at the door. I would later find out that a few weeks earlier, my stepfather, who had major gambling and drinking problems, had gone on a bender at the casino and lost a bunch of money while heavily drunk. He'd then broken into a local home, burglarized it while a young child witnessed the event, and taken all that stuff back to our house. I don't think any of our Christmas presents had stolen items in them, but it embarrassed us to see the cops come and unwrap all the gifts under the tree to determine what he did and did not steal. Come to find out, it was actually really stupid shit that he stole, and it made no sense to me, but I guess when you're drunk, rationality goes out the door.

To this day, I cringe thinking of that experience. I still think about my sister at such a young age watching the police open her presents. I could never imagine putting my daughter or son through that. It's because of my stepdad that I rarely drink and don't step foot into a casino unless it's to get to a hotel.

I only knew my real dad until I was around eleven years old. That's when he went to prison. To be honest, my dad didn't work—at least not in what would normally be considered a respectable job. Looking back on it, I can now see how my dad afforded decent Christmas presents, had nice stuff, and did all the things he did. Drug dealing, among other things, is "profitable." It's not like we lived in luxury or anything like that, but dang, for Christmas, my mom and dad definitely blessed us. Unfortunately, it came at great expense.

Believe it or not, my dad going to prison was probably the best thing that ever happened to me at the time. I don't mean I'm happy he went to prison. I wish he didn't have to, but there's a good chance I could have ended up like him otherwise. Had he continued that life and remained a present figure while I grew up, I honestly don't know where I'd be.

Growing up without a respectable father figure presented some great challenges. On our weekends with our father, my sister and I spent most of the time sitting on the steps, waiting for him to show up. Sometimes he did, but on those occasions that he didn't, it crushed us. I still think about that little boy and girl sitting on the stairs. It's like a bad dream that just keeps playing over and over in my head. A constant reminder of what not to do. That episode became the driving reason why I put in so much effort with my own children. I never want them to feel what I felt, but I also understand that simply giving them things or using money to appease them won't truly make them happy. My time with them can be enough.

One day, my dad came to visit— for the last time in a long time. He pulled up in a Chevy Nova and took us to Dairy Queen. As we sat there, he told us that he had to go away for a while, and we couldn't see him other than during prison visitation. In response, my sister and I began crying.

After that initial sadness, I became mad and resented him so much that I wouldn't answer the phone if I knew he was calling, and I'd decline to go visit him. I wish someone had talked to me at the time and shown me how to be rational and pick up that phone call. Something as simple as understanding that people make mistakes.

That altered my life. It could have altered it for good. Looking back, I knew that I would have to make the best of it. I had a great mom, but losing my dad due to his criminal activity wrecked me. Would I become a statistic? When my dad got caught up in dealing weed and money laundering and who knows what else, he was locked up for the next five years—well into my high school years. Just like that, I was on my own. Surely, destiny meant I'd find trouble, right? Statistics love to tell you how shitty you will be if you don't have a father, but statistics can't account for the drive and heart of an underdog. I'm a living example. The odds suggested that I should have wound up in prison, gotten involved in drugs, and generally wasted my life. To put it bluntly, screw statistics.

That pain and sadness made me stronger. My father wouldn't be the last person to let me down, but I realized early on that not only could I survive those bitter disappointments, but I could actually use them to my advantage. It's not easy or intuitive to learn a lesson like that. It's really not fair, but then again, life is not fair. I simply had to look at myself and realize that I could count on myself to either let me down or succeed. And that's it. Now, don't get me wrong—there were other people in life whom I could depend on. However, I could 100 percent rely on myself to do one of two things: push forward or not.

I also learned early on how to really look at some of these bad things and recognize they couldn't get much worse. For example, if my current situation represented the bottom, then I could only go up from there. I know that's a simplistic way to say it, but that's really how I felt watching my father leave for prison. Despite the other devastating hardships I endured in my life, which I will discuss later, nothing was as bad as my dad exiting my life because I essentially became numb to other negative feelings. Maybe that wasn't a good thing, but it helped my mindset of thinking it couldn't get any worse. If it did get worse, I reminded myself I'd made it through the last thing, and I'd make it to the next.

I still do my best to look for the good in people, but I also know that we should expect that we'll get the worst sometimes. Now that I am a father myself, I am determined not to make the mistakes I saw mine make growing up. Of course, no one is going to be perfect. I certainly am not, but I have always strived to do my best and give my children the time that they need. My real dad came late to the party, but I'm grateful he eventually figured it out and became a positive influence in my life. Better late than never, right?

I didn't understand why my dad and mom weren't together. My mother preferred for me to have her maiden name, Olson, as my last name. I only knew, or thought, that I had a dad who didn't seem to care much about me or my sister. However, when my dad did pick us up, and we got to spend time with that side of the family, I was happy to live as a Diaz for the weekend. For those periods of time, it felt like I had a dad again and was a part of his family, even if for only a short while.

Eventually, I would go home to my stepdad, but it just wasn't the same, as he brought drama to my family. It wasn't always like that though. At first, it satisfied us that he had his own demons to fight, but unfortunately, my sister and I bore the brunt of it.

As much as I managed to avoid becoming a statistic, one did turn out to affect me. I experienced abuse and neglect, and as a young adolescent, I endured sexual abuse. I've only told a handful of people before writing this book because, at the time, the horror of other kids knowing that about me seemed absolutely devastating. I had already faced such a hard phase in my life; the last thing I needed was to deal with mean kids. To make matters worse, it was a male family member who forced himself on me, creating my first sexual experience. I still don't understand why he did it. It didn't make sense to me then, and it doesn't make sense to me now.

My own experiences have clearly played a role in how protective I am of my daughter and son today. I do worry that I can be overprotective and do my best to ensure I don't shelter them too much from the world, but it's challenging. I've found it incredibly hard to let them spend the night at a friend's house or just go out and about. Of course, I know the people they're with, but do I really know them? My experience made me extremely cautious.

I went from collecting Pogs (a game collecting milk caps), playing pickup hockey, and doing other kid things to sex and all the things that come with it. In addition to the molestation, I was exposed to pornography at a young age, and that alone is the destroyer of all expectations when it comes to what intimacy in life should be. Once you are exposed to something, it's hard to walk back from that. I was young, vulnerable, and unable to defend myself. I had no idea what was happening. For a time, I blocked it out completely, but as I've learned to heal, I still recognize it's something that will always be there.

As you can tell by now, this book is not just cool war stories. My combat missions are front and center, but I could perform at the highest ability with SEAL Team ▉ because of everything I overcame before I got there. Those stories are what made the cool war stories possible.

How does a child overcome being sexually abused? There's no easy answer, at least not one that I've found. It's difficult, and everyone is different. What works for one person might not work for another. The first thing I did was tell the girl who was my best friend. I got it out there. It may not have been an adult, but still, I told someone, so it no longer remained a secret. I knew in my heart that what had happened was wrong. I also knew that this did not make me a bad person or unworthy of being saved by Jesus. I had my faith and someone to talk to, and those two things helped me push through. For a long time, I wondered if God had punished me for something I'd done by putting my abuser in my path. However, I learned long ago that it's not God but rather man's own sin that causes bad things like that to happen.

In addition, I've found that holding stuff in only makes things worse. It can hurt and be messy, but confronting issues head on has prevented them from affecting other parts of my life. I should have told more people—at least that's what I tell myself now. Back then, it wasn't so easy, and I didn't consider who else might fall victim to his sexual abuse. So who knows how many other kids or boys he touched? It's really bullshit looking back on it to see what he did to me.

My family will read this and may find some of it shocking. My dad, in particular, may find much of this hurtful. I do truly love my father, but still, I wanted to become everything he wasn't. For instance, I always wanted to become a police officer—the exact opposite of my father. You can choose your own outcome. I knew that I wanted to help others and lock up bad people. I'm not talking about the people who just smoke some weed. I never cared about that. I'm talking about the really bad people. Obviously, I never became a cop, but I did join the navy and wound up hunting down bad guys, so my path in life turned out pretty similar to what I thought it might become when I was a kid.

When my dad left, I continued on the same track of caring for myself and pushing forward. I had odd jobs like mowing lawns but worked for others starting at thirteen when I got a job pushing carts for Cub Foods. We tried to always fill the cart room because as long as the cart room stayed full, management left us alone. I tried hard at that job and wanted to become a supervisor in the maintenance department. At fifteen, I got that promotion. I wasn't even old enough to drive, yet I led other youths and even some adults. They didn't like that, but that's on them. Shame on them for giving and accepting the minimum in life. I wanted more, so I worked for it.

I relied on my own willpower to get to move up. South St. Paul to being selected to serve with the SEAL teams. Go figure the odds of that happening. I never quit after a hard time. I took the hard times as life lessons and took failures as a chance to make a positive impact. Even to this day, as difficult as life seems, I always try to find the positives in those lessons.

Don't believe me? Here's a failure for you. At seventeen, I joined the National Guard while still in high school. I did that because I saw the

cool Army National Guard videos. When I found out that they probably wouldn't send me to fight overseas, I wanted out. We had just entered
Afghanistan, and I wanted to help people. What better way to rid the world
of trash? Little did I know the National Guard could deploy, but I had no
one to guide me. So I told my National Guard staff sergeant that I would
not return because I wanted to join the Army and deploy overseas. They
fought me on it, and he said I would never amount to anything.

By the way, never be the adult telling some kid that they won't amount
to anything. I still remember that guy to this day. I wasn't going to let him
tell me I wouldn't achieve anything in my life. I wish I could find that dude
and say thank you. Thank you for being ignorant because I'm the last person anyone should doubt. I don't mean to come across as arrogant. There's
a difference between cocky and confident. We underdogs have to dig deep
and find that confidence.

My family planned to move to Alabama after I graduated high school,
and I desired a new start. I hadn't thought that far ahead when I took the
oath of enlistment that locked me into the National Guard. I simply said I
wasn't coming back. They called me a loser and gave me an RE-3 discharge,
meaning I wouldn't be eligible for continued Army service. Real nice. What
a great way to motivate a senior in high school. My God, I was so wrong for
the way I handled that situation. It's not an excuse, but I had no role models,
and so I failed. Surely that would end my military career, right? Wrong!

As my next tentative step, I applied to Inver Hills Community College.
I didn't bother applying to four-year schools, assuming they wouldn't admit
me or that I couldn't handle the courses. I had low self-esteem. Really crappy
self-esteem. No one in my family had attended college, and all worked fac-
tory jobs, so naturally, college was never pushed on me. I'm kind of happy
about that to be honest. There are a lot of excellent jobs that don't require a
college degree. Anyway, I ultimately chose the U.S. Navy.

I met my recruiter, Chief Petty Officer Karst, while in high school.
He treated me well and didn't pressure me to join. I told him no initially
because of the ordeal with the National Guard. Well, a year later, guess who

was surprised as hell to see me? Chief Karst. I begged him to let me in. I just wanted to serve and do something that was above myself. To serve others.

Also, in my experience, community college felt just like high school. It didn't offer me much more than I already had. For instance, I took a sociology inequalities class taught by a feminist that seemed to only focus on why the white man oppresses. Being white and Hispanic, I didn't understand the negative outlook. My mother did a great job of raising me and taught me to treat everyone fairly and equally. A person's sex, color, or whatever didn't matter to me and didn't affect how I treated them. Then and now, it's all about how they are as a human being. Nowadays, it's okay to just use that negative mentality toward other races. I assumed I wouldn't find that attitude in the military, and that helped point me in that direction. Blame the man. I'm not saying our country doesn't have problems, but at some point, we have to move forward.

The USA is a mix of different races, religions, etc., and I think people forget that. The navy showed me that. It showed me men, women, black, Hispanic, white could all come together, and no one cared because we all did the same shit. Sure, the navy has a few of these problems. There's racism, sexism, and all the other -isms, but I surrounded myself with good people. I had joined a new family—one that would last a lifetime. A real brotherhood.

Of course, the National Guard didn't do me any favors when it came to applying for the U.S. Navy. Although many wouldn't even try after my disqualifying discharge, I went to meet with the commanding officer of the recruiting district. Not by choice—I needed him to sign off on allowing me in. It was up to him.

He said, "Why should I let you in my navy?"

"Sir, I won't disappoint you," I responded.

I'd never wanted something so much in my life, and he must have sensed my sincerity. So he signed the papers to let me in. My brief stint in the National Guard could have derailed my entire military career, but I didn't let it. I fought for what I wanted and stayed the course.

We're all going to fail in life. Life has its disappointments, but how we deal with those failures and letdowns will lead to success if we learn from what happened and make the appropriate changes. If I had let being molested, growing up without a father, or the National Guard guy calling me a loser define who I was, then I wouldn't have made it anywhere.

I absolutely believe that losing and suffering setbacks allowed me to look where I went wrong in life. It made me examine my role in things and recognize where I was at fault but also where I wasn't. For example, it wasn't my fault that someone molested me, and it wasn't my fault that I had an absent father. However, I took responsibility for mistakes like the National Guard episode. In that case, I should have asked the important questions to understand all the ramifications of what I was signing up for. I failed, but I chose to use that experience as a chance to learn so that I would do better next time.

We must find that grit. I've found it through steadfastly navigating through challenging situations. I didn't know it then, but this grit I developed would ultimately save my life.

CHAPTER 4
ACCELERATE YOUR LIFE

This book is a bit different from other books by SEALs. Readers won't find stories about Basic Underwater Demolition/SEAL training (BUD/S), surf torture, drownproofing, or chasing the elusive Trident. That's because I held a different specialty. I wasn't looking to pursue that kind of life. Little did I know I'd come closer than I ever expected. The U.S. Navy used the slogan "Accelerate Your Life" at the time, so I supposed I would soon get that acceleration. I did briefly consider taking the PT challenge test in boot camp to go to BUD/S, but the fire to do it just didn't burn in me. Shocking, right? Considering where I ended up, you'd think that I would have at least tried. I wanted to get into the navy, do my time, and get out as fast as I could. I had a plan to use my navy experience in the criminal justice field in some capacity in Minnesota.

On 9/11, as a high school senior, I remember sitting in class at Dakota County Technical College (partnering with our high school) pursuing criminal justice courses with the hope of joining the police force. By the time the TV turned on, the first plane had hit the first tower, and shortly after, the second plane hit the second tower. We didn't do much that morning other than helplessly watch the events taking place in real, vivid time. I had only heard about terrorism a couple of years before in high school. That day gave me one of my main motivations for joining the military. I knew I could make a difference regarding the War on Terror, and the U.S. Navy would ultimately provide me with that opportunity.

I'd left everything back at home, and after my mom left for Alabama, I really didn't have much. All my friends went off to college, and I went to Inver Hills Community College. Community college or college in general works for many. I just think had I known what I know now, I may not have done that. I actually think college for some people is a waste. If we had more job-shadowing opportunities such as apprenticeships, a lot of people probably wouldn't spend the amount of money on college classes they do. Realistically, a lot of people just don't need to. I also learned I could make six figures training dogs, and that doesn't require a degree. I didn't want to take on massive debt before I even landed a job.

When my mom left, I ended up living in a couple of places, including my aunt's house. Although it was nice of her to offer me a place to stay, I wanted to live closer to school, so I moved into this apartment complex next to the college. The run-down place had a shared kitchen, and I had one room in the three-bedroom apartment. I often wondered if I'd encounter a drug deal or get mugged. But I couldn't afford much more at the time, as I was working at Target. I struggled during that year of my life, but the experience I gained would prove hugely important later. After living in that crap apartment, the stuff I went through in boot camp seemed like paradise because they required every swinging dick in my division to have the same amount of room storing their shit or making their bed.

The U.S. Navy accepted me into the Delayed Entry Program in December of 2002 with a ship date of August 25 the following year. That program served a few functions, such as reserving a spot in a desired school after boot camp or allowing a sailor to begin their reserve time. Most think of military enlistments as lasting four years, but the military also requires additional years of standby reserve duty. For the next several months, I counted down the days.

Each day brought me one day closer to getting the hell out of Minnesota and forging my own path. Those several months seemed hard for a variety of reasons. First, I found it tough to wait for something I wanted so badly. Second, I had begun a personal relationship with a girlfriend whom I really cared about. She wasn't like other girls who had an attitude and were all about flash. We worked together at Target, which is where we originally met, and we had a really great relationship. I didn't want to leave because I knew we wouldn't survive a separation. She'd soon graduate from high school and move on to do better things.

Just for reference, that was my old way of thinking. I typically felt pessimistic about things in life because nothing seemed to go the way I had intended. So I figured she would go off to college and eventually get tired of us living fairly close to each other but not close enough to see each other every day.

On the evening of August 23, 2003, I spent the night at the local Marriott where my recruiter would take us to a Military Entrance Processing Station (MEPS) and then to the bus that would take us to the airport. I learned that sometimes we must sacrifice the things we care about, and that's okay because there are better things to come. We don't have to always know the plan.

If I had stayed in Minnesota, I might have turned out fine, but then I wouldn't have wound up with the SEAL teams—a truly life-altering experience. If I hadn't joined, I wouldn't have met the people I have in my life now. I wouldn't have met my wife, Erica, which means I wouldn't have my two children, Jacob and Emma, in my life. The idea of a world without them just makes me sick. So, yeah, sometimes giving up what we know for the unknown is hard, but I think it's worth the risk. That unknown could turn out terrible, but it could also turn out better than we could have ever imagined. I'll take that chance every time.

After the night at the Marriott, I knew the vacation had ended. When we landed in Chicago, a group of recruit division commanders (RDCs), which are the U.S. Navy drill instructors, took us to the buses where they promptly slapped us with a dose of reality. The myriad of commands and "what the hells" came one after another. I sat there asking myself what I had gotten myself into. You see videos of boot camp prior to going in, but until you get there and you are in it, you can't really know how challenging it's going to be.

The amount of pressure they put on recruits is extraordinary. I don't know what today's boot camp is like, but I can tell you that some of the situations I found myself in while serving, especially combat, were incredibly stressful. We were often faced with life-and-death decisions. It made me appreciate why they treated us the way they did during boot camp when we were preparing for what was to come. It would be easy to look at all the yelling and lack of sleep combined with constant physical and mental challenges that threatened to overwhelm us as abuse or hazing. All that may have been tough, but it served a purpose.

I've never been on a "boat," but I've heard people who have talked about it. Yes, younger sailors called it a boat, but the crusty old-timers corrected us to call it a ship. When a ship goes to general quarters or battle stations, that shit is no joke, and the last thing they want is someone who can't handle themselves under pressure.

I remember being in a firefight overseas in some compound. A fully loaded PKM machine gun lit up the courtyard. Bullets flew everywhere, but our team kept pushing. The amount of sheer butthole-puckering I was doing was intense, but regardless of whether I shat myself, I kept moving. I kept moving for the guys to the right and left of me. Was it scary? Yes. But what mattered was that we kept doing our job after we got past the fear. Fight or flight.

That's what I would learn, but I didn't know what the hell to expect when still in boot camp. They attempt to ratchet up the tension, but how could anyone truly understand combat until they experienced it? The following story explains why they do this.

———————

You're going to hear plenty of combat stories in this book, but one stands out as a good example. In 2011, I served in Afghanistan for what would be my last deployment with the SEAL teams. On this particular mission, our leaders told us it would be an ass-kicker, but I don't think anyone expected how it would inevitably turn out. I don't remember how many kilometers we traveled, but the vertical hike up and back down the mountain really brought on the pain. Such mean, gnarly terrain. We started our infil (infiltration or entering point) by landing in a small field, and then we began walking toward this mountain. I remember thinking we could straight line it to the target. That would have been fine with me because I didn't need the extra exercise.

I walked up front with Brando, one of the dogs I worked with during the course of my time with the SEAL Teams. That put me just behind several shooters and the snipers. Step by step, we made our way up the mountain. We climbed over dirt and rocks, then down a dip before tackling the next uphill section. The higher we climbed, the more vertical the mountain became. It didn't matter—we pushed through to our objective.

A couple of the guys stopped to take a breath, signaling me to keep going. Our reconnaissance (RECCE) snipers moved out in front, so I followed them with Brando. Every once in a while, I would need to hand Brando up to someone because of the height of the climb. But it wasn't always as simple as that. Sometimes I would need to attach my ten-foot line to him and throw it up to one of the guys because Brando was just too damn big to lift up that high. Little by little, we continued, and I stopped for a second to rest with one of the guys.

He looked at me. "How the hell are you not tired?

I absolutely was tired, and my hips were on fire. This particular operation occurred after my major injury, and I now had metal rods in my legs, but no way would I admit to feeling it. I wasn't a SEAL, and I needed them to know that I could keep up regardless. I'd joined them on that mission to provide support, and I was determined to do just that. I also knew that any failure of mine would almost certainly get me shitcanned from the command and sent back to resume normal MA duties. I wouldn't allow that, nor would I fail myself or anyone else for that matter. So I kept up.

Somewhere on that hike, I lost my super cool Winkler knife. That shit pissed me off. It had a black steel blade, three inches long, with a black handle and could cut through some of the thickest materials like butter. Winkler made some of the best knives I've ever owned. Funny the things that you remember. I'm sure some person over in Afghanistan has it now. Might as well be the Taliban since they have all our shit now anyways.

It was still nighttime as we approached the top of that shitty mountain, and I was definitely exhausted. Another team intended to join us. Our plan required us to hike in a small force and then surround the compound while the rest of the team flew in on another helicopter.

At some point during the hike, the team discussed turning back. It had nothing to do with giving up but rather realizing that the difficult terrain might delay the time we would get to the target, and we'd lose most of the advantage due to the daylight. Of course, we didn't turn back. We found a way, and after all that effort, it was way more fun to hit a target than to simply return to base. So we climbed and climbed until we got to what I thought had to be the top—but we'd only made it to another ridge of another peak, so on we went.

We finally made it to the other side. The downside was even more difficult. My legs were toast, and the rocks were jagged. At that point, I would have been happy just falling down the hill to the bottom, but alas, that was not an option. We made it down and set containment on the building. At that time, they called in the rest of the assault force to land near the target. Almost as soon as that happened, we encountered gunfire from the compound, a rather large area that the enemy used to train and house fighters.

The rest of the assault force came up after the CH-47s took off, and I remember a couple of guys walking up to me, saying, "Damn, you look like shit." It was no wonder—I had spent most of my time lifting Brando and then climbing on my hands and knees up a rocky slope. It had truly been a full-body workout.

Our leader made the decision to do a callout of the compound after the quick first engagement, and only a few came out. We made entry in the courtyard and found a trench had been dug or was naturally made. Next thing I knew, a PKM cut loose and unleashed hell from a doorway across the way. We engaged and kept at it until the shooting had stopped. I thought for sure one of our guys had been hit. Lucky for me, I was able to grab a sliver of a building and some large rocks for cover. It wasn't much, but it served its purpose.

After all the racket, it became eerily quiet. Moments later, we made the call to pull out of the compound. We'd killed a lot of people in the initial firefight in the courtyard. The situation was crap. The only options were to go in and lose a bunch of guys to some people who didn't matter or to simply back off and do other things. We chose the latter. They were dug in like the ticks they were, and to this day, because of politics, I'm surprised that we were allowed to take the next step: bomb the shit out of that compound.

We called in the high-mobility artillery rocket system (HIMARS), which was mounted to a truck, and unloaded on the building. Munition after munition dropped on that compound. We had to climb partway back up that big-ass mountain while the munitions fell and helicopters fired rockets on the building. We then came back down and made entry on the compound—or what remained of it.

I have no idea how someone could survive that, but believe it or not, one person remained alive after it was all said and done. Lo and behold, an elderly man with a dog walked out of one of the buildings that partially remained. I honestly felt bad for him, but at the same time, he had harbored all of those assholes or Taliban in training. If his hearing wasn't trash before, it sure was afterwards.

I sent Brando in to search for people while the other dog worked in another area of the building. Methodically, like every other time we approached a target, we moved in with the team and continued sending Brando into different areas so he could search. He would end up clearing the buildings but only finding dead people—still a win for the dog and a win for us because that confirmed only dead men remained. We would eventually get to the end of the compound and find a pair of shoes on the ground as if somebody had been blown right out of them. I'd say you have to be kind of twisted for thinking it, but part of me found that hilarious. Like they say, play stupid games, win stupid prizes.

Back in 2003, when I was being yelled at in boot camp, I didn't know anything about combat and certainly had no idea what I would later face on that mission with Brando. I had my hands full following orders that the RDCs barked at us from every direction.

On the first day, they sent us into a hall with telephones where they gave us only a moment to call our parents, tell them we'd made it, and say goodbye. That's it. The process seemed absolutely crazy for someone like me who had lacked an authority figure, but it proved a wonderful awakening. I would soon thrive off that shit, but not until I broke a little.

Sometime during the first day or so, they marched us into a room with every other recruit and told us to take all our shit off and put it in a bag. Everything! So there I stood, bare-ass naked, before I put on a pair of U.S. Navy sweatpants and a sweatshirt—my standard attire for the next few weeks. Every other person there with me donned the same gear. Then, my street clothes were sent back to my mom in a bag. Apparently, it looked like I'd packed in a hurry because she found them all balled up. Well, she was right.

When the RDCs asked me to jump, I didn't ask how high—I simply jumped. A few days into it, I finally broke down a bit. I started hyperventilating and crying and thought I was having a heart attack. No heart attack though. I was simply reacting to the most stress I had ever experienced in my life.

Since I had grown up without a male authority figure, no one had ever yelled at me except my mother, and even then, it had been just enough to keep me straight and in line. Both her discipline and that from the boot camp RDCs really prepared me for times later in life when I'd deal with actual stress—things that were life and death.

But that day, as the RDCs sat there yelling at me and mocking me, I couldn't catch my breath. One RDC, a chief petty officer, came over and told them to get the hell off of me. And they did. Those five minutes allowed me to get grounded again. From that moment on, I told myself I'd never let anyone make me cry. I pledged to remain stronger. I know that incident made my personality harder than any time before.

For the next several weeks, we learned to work as a team. It made for a great process because we all came from different backgrounds, which also allowed us a chance to learn about someone else's life. We had this one guy from Africa who had been rolled back a couple of times, but he refused to give up. Similar to holding back a student in school, an RDC can send a recruit back one class if that recruit lacks the physical fitness requirements, mentally fails to comply, or has suffered an injury. No one wanted to get rolled back, so I appreciated that guy's tenacity. Plus, I learned a valuable lesson from one of my RDCs that we don't give up on anyone. As long as we worked hard and were willing to put in the work to graduate, we'd make it—even that guy. I don't think I've ever seen anyone happier than him when he graduated.

Learning to eat the navy way presented another challenge that's hard for those who have never enjoyed eight weeks in boot camp to understand. I stood last in line when we marched to the chow hall the first time. I literally had five minutes to suck down all my food. We constantly stayed on the move, so we always felt hungry. They fed us well, but man, did I feel like I could just eat and eat.

Near the end of boot camp, our RDC laid out a challenge for us. Whoever aced the last test would get all three days of liberty when we graduated. My girlfriend planned to come, and I wanted to see her badly. Little did I know that would probably be the last time I'd see her as "my girlfriend." I studied my ass off for that test. Any notes I took, I read over and over. I guess when you're young and in love, or so you think, you'll do damn near anything. The test came, and they posted the results. I made 100 percent and got that liberty.

Soon after graduating, I'd be off to the initial school (called "A" school) for master-at-arms (the navy term for military police and abbreviated as MA). The whole reason I'd joined the military was so that I could be a police officer, and that was the same reason I'd taken college classes. Minnesota had passed a law that if you served as a military police officer—or, in my case, an MA—you could take the test to become a police officer in Minnesota after four years of service. That is exactly why I chose that military specialty, and I figured it would be a quick in and out—or so I thought.

The U.S. Navy trained MAs in one of two places. One was Lackland Air Force Base. Notice the words Air Force in that sentence. They had nice dorm rooms with wonderful Air Force chow halls. There's a running joke that the Air Force does it right. They spend the money on all the good, comfy stuff and then come back and say they need more for the mission.

The other school was in Joint Expeditionary Base (JEB) Little Creek where they would bus us out to the local schoolhouse. That area of land that consists of both Fort Story and Little Creek dates back to the late seventeenth century when Jamestown settlers sailed nearby, searching for a settlement. The military also heavily used it during World War II, and in my time, I've seen it used as a base for multiple commands, namely afloat commands.

Guess what option I got? Option mutha F'in B. No Air Force chow hall. No comfy barracks. Just some old-ass navy barracks, and we were served dinner at the schoolhouse. I charitably call it food. I guess I can't really complain. They kept me fed, and for that, I'm grateful.

I arrived at JEB Little Creek ready and eager to learn something. Unfortunately, the U.S. Navy held a negative attitude toward allowing junior sailors to become an MA. Prior to 2002 or so, candidates had to hold at least an E-5 paygrade to become an MA. The average sailor typically earned E-5 at the end of their first enlistment or the beginning of their second. However, after 9/11, the U.S. Navy needed to up its manning in the

MA rating with a goal of ten thousand MAs. That's why I was eligible and why some of the old hands weren't happy about it. I could see their point. I'm sure that by allowing a ton of young people in that job, they were bound to have issues, but I didn't care what anyone thought. I went there to learn.

We had a real jerk as our chief in charge. He was disrespectful at the very least. If you assume I'm just bitching because I didn't like a senior leader being tough, think again. I'd become that leader one day, and watching that chief act that way ingrained in me what not to do and how not to treat people. One can lead and earn respect without acting like a total asshole. And before anyone thinks that I was too sensitive to being led or whatever you want to call it, I did meet really great leaders in my career. As a chief myself, I simply knew that whatever I did had a reason. This chief operating the way he did had no meaning to it. Almost like a bully in school who is allowed to just get away with whatever they want. I kept hoping I'd find some decency in that asshole chief. Some people love the feeling of power. I love the feeling of the team.

This guy was the senior enlisted leader at the schoolhouse, so I guess you could say he did what he wanted. That was okay by me. I could absolutely learn from that example. I could see a rough few weeks ahead of me, but I'd survived boot camp, and that gave me confidence. I kept telling myself: *The only person holding you back is yourself. Plain and simple. It's just yourself.* People often want to find excuses for not making their dreams come true, whatever those may be. But I promise you, if it's a realistic dream, keep chasing.

I don't have as many crazy training stories as some of the SEALs I worked with who endured BUD/S and got to do all that cool training. A typical day in MA school consisted of the following: I would wake up in the morning for some sort of physical training with the whole class. After breakfast, we trudged outside our main building for buses that would take us over to a contracted training school out in town. We learned everything from weapons training all the way to the rules and regulations of the U.S. Navy or the Uniform Code of Military Justice. We focused more on book learning than realistic scenario training, although I know now that they teach active shooter drills and other more advanced drills. Then, it was lunch, more classroom learning, and more training, so I just tried to get through the day.

I ultimately wanted to get to my new command where we would at least get better training more geared to the actual work we'd be doing. The MA school focused on basic law enforcement, but over in Bahrain, it was all force protection that combined three elements: antiterrorism, physical security, and law enforcement. There, MAs would stand at the gates and prevent unauthorized access to the installation.

I think at some point the chief realized my commitment to doing the best I could, and he laid off me. When he asked me about my choice for duty stations, I asked him where I'd learn the most about my job and maybe get to deploy. I think that impressed him. He stated I'd get the experience I needed for force protection in Bahrain.

We had three slots for us to put our preferred choice, although the navy would send us wherever they needed us most. Everyone else chose locations like Italy, Japan, and other places. I put down Bahrain three times. I remained adamant about learning my job and going somewhere to do something actionable. Orders came in, and some of us ended up getting Bahrain while others celebrated their choices. I think some people couldn't understand why I wanted Bahrain. But at that time, I never wavered from wanting to work as far away from Minnesota as possible. Bahrain was damn near the other side of the world from Minnesota, so off to Bahrain went!

CHAPTER 5

TO PROTECT AND SERVE

In December of 2003, I graduated from MA "A" School in Little Creek, Virginia. I'd soon get my wish and head for Bahrain—the toughest duty station that the navy had to offer for MAs. I'd taken it to heart when that chief had told me if I wanted to really succeed, Bahrain was the place to start. I think initially he had the impression that I was just another young kid that he'd have to graduate before moving on to the next. It was good to see that he, in the end, saw me for who I was and realized that I really wanted this. Plus, I wanted to be near the action.

I'd have a rinse and repeat attitude throughout my naval career. For example, I remember standing in a dealership in Inver Grove Heights, Minnesota, in March of 2003 when we first went into Iraq, telling myself that I needed to go and serve where they needed me most. This theme drove all my decisions throughout my career.

After MA school graduation, I returned home for a couple of weeks to see family as well as my girlfriend for what would be the last time. It's crazy, but most people don't believe it when people say relationships don't last in the military. I'll be the first to admit that marriage is difficult, but leaving my girlfriend for my naval adventure certainly wasn't a recipe for marital or relationship success. I looked at the bigger picture though and thought to myself that if our relationship was meant to be, then it would work itself out. If not, then so be it. I accepted that.

I landed in Bahrain on my birthday, December 30, 2003. At that point, I had never even traveled outside of the country and had only seen two different states out of fifty in my whole lifetime. We arrived to warm temperatures, but it wasn't incredibly hot. Of course, everything looked different. The buildings, the people, the roads, everything seemed different.

We assumed we'd be housed in some barracks or other military-like housing. For a moment, we thought we were in the Air Force because the U.S. Navy put us up in a five-star hotel with a roommate. From there, they shuttled us back and forth from the hotel to the base every day until we either had rooms in the barracks or rooms out in town.

They soon realized they would not have enough room on the base, so they provided us with a housing allowance for living out in town. Not a terrible way to start my time in the navy. However, that soon became trouble for some who couldn't handle the responsibility. Give young people that amount of money for the first time they're out on their own, throw into the mix clubs like the bar called Rock Bottom, and you can only guess what would happen. They certainly found themselves at rock bottom one way or another. Plenty of us managed to control those newfound freedoms, but it proved too tempting for a few.

I arrived on the base the first time in awe of the walls, the security, and everything about it. Amazing! MAs rarely used police cars or needed to pull people over or any of that. When a big ship like an aircraft carrier pulled in, we'd see some action from all the sailors fighting and partying at the base Desert Dome.

A few days after arriving at the base, I saw the military working dogs sweeping the vehicles for explosives out front. Those vehicles or buses shuttled kids back and forth from home to school. This particular school was for Department of Defense employees' dependents but also for some kids local to Bahrain. From that moment, I knew I wanted to be a part of that.

I didn't have a love for dogs growing up; the ones we owned annoyed the crap out of me, and for the most part, we had simply inherited a couple of them. However, this one instance totally transformed the trajectory of my career.

I had asked some of the leadership there how to become a dog handler. They told me I first had to do well at my current job and prove excellence as an MA before looking at other options. Of course, you know that wasn't good enough for me and my timeline for wanting to do awesome things. I don't know if it's simply in my nature, but I have always looked for the next best thing or the next thing that can make me the best at what I'm doing.

Soon after, I went through base indoctrination and Naval Security Force Academy. The security department then placed me in a section. We essentially worked port and starboard duty, twelve hours on and twelve hours off. We worked nearly every day because they were so undermanned, so we welcomed the occasional day off. However, I didn't mind the constant work that much, and I think, for the most part, it kept me out of trouble.

While most used their day off to go home and sleep after those long hours of gate duty, I chose to go down to the kennel and ask how I could volunteer. I could only do this on my time off so I wouldn't risk getting in trouble with patrols for taking time away from that. The kennel said I could come for a couple of hours after my shift but stressed that this had to be on my own time, and I made sure that I complied.

At first, I mainly cleaned up dog poop, washed out kennels, fed the dogs, and did whatever work needed to be done. Later, I put on the bite suit and served time as the bite dummy. Looking back on that, it probably wasn't a good idea since I had no experience with catching dogs in a bite suit. It did require a certain set of skills so that we didn't hurt ourselves or the dog. I remained exhausted but wanted to prove my interest. I would return home, get about five or six hours of sleep, and then make the hour and a half commute before my shift. I continued to learn the lesson that if I really wanted something, I had to go out and get it. No one would simply give it to me, and I knew I shouldn't expect them to.

Those hard days included a few haters. Some people assumed I thought I was better than them because I spent time at the kennel. It's not like I tried to skirt my gate guard duties or made them cover for me. I couldn't understand their resentment at me wanting to explore other opportunities. It was simply something I wanted to do. Because of the extra hours I spent, I had my personal qualification standards (PQS) signed off probably quicker than most. I really wanted to work in that kennel as a dog handler.

The navy would label some of the things the kennel had me do as hazing. I would like to think of it more as a rite of passage. The truth was some people needed to toughen up just a little bit.

When I would come down to the kennel, the leaders of the kennel would make me do things like "walk my dog." That doesn't sound like a bad thing, but in this case, my dog was an ammo can. I had to tie a leash on it and tell people its name. A little embarrassing but all in good fun.

They would also make me clean the nastiest kennels where dogs would paint the hell out of them. You read that right—paint. We had dogs that would literally take their own poop, play with it, and then paint the walls with it. Regular modern-day, four-pawed Picassos. Nothing better than walking into the kennel knowing you're going to not only have to clean them but also give dogs baths so that they can ride around in a patrol car. They knew what the dogs did, and guess who would be the one to clean up the mess? Me. I'd get locked in a kennel and sprayed down with the water hose, but again, all just a bunch of people having fun. If it had really bothered me, I wouldn't have wanted to come back.

All these things were okay because working as a dog handler would require me to endure a lot of stress. If I could not handle just a little bit of "hazing," I'd find it much harder working a dog. I remember so many times when my dog would mess up in a training scenario and my frustration would build. I had to find some way to dig deep, get out of my own head, and make it work.

Some senior leaders actually questioned me about hazing I might have done to others after I became a dog handler. As a seaman, E-3 paygrade,

I'm not sure how they thought I could haze anyone. A seaman ranks near the bottom in the navy. They brought up the same type of hazing I described above. I only told them what had happened to me but explained that I had no problem with it. No physical harm had come to me or anyone else. Maybe a guy or two had some hurt feelings, but when things get hard, life doesn't give a damn about feelings. We were serving in the military, not at some damn flower shop or fast-food joint. People would go to war and have their stress put to the ultimate test. If they could be broken under the littlest of pressure from a harmless prank, then they should choose another line of work. In general, I tried not to let myself become offended.

I now had my PQS signed, which basically meant that I knew how to do the job, I had put in the work, and the command leadership thought I could move on to the next thing. If I would have stayed in patrols, I would have continued on a normal MA trajectory, but I wanted to work at the kennel full time—even if that meant being kennel support and putting up with all the bullshit. Because with that bullshit came knowledge. I learned so much from all those handlers because they had spent a long time in the navy and knew how to handle dogs as well as anyone. I remember one always addressed me as Prospect. To this day, I still have disagreements with him on social media, but I'll never forget the stuff that he taught me.

I finally won acceptance into the kennel full time. A bittersweet moment as I watched people I had come over on the plane with to serve as MAs continue going out on patrols while I had earned the right to do something I loved. I would still see them on occasion but looked forward to the path that would lead me to a different place.

As I finished my last patrol shift, my chief petty officer came over the radio and said that I would be going 10-7 (out of service) from patrols down to the kennel. I remember that moment so vividly because I did not expect him to do that. At the time, it represented somebody acknowledging everything that I had done up to that point to work in the dog kennel while also performing all those hours on patrols. It validated my worthiness to move on to the next challenge in the military working dog program.

For the next several months, I would spend most of my days either cleaning kennels, training, or doing whatever I could to earn a spot in dog school. The command, Naval Support Activity Bahrain, agreed to pay for me to attend dog school in exchange for my service in the kennel. In return, I would have to serve an extra year in Bahrain. The relationship with my girlfriend had ended as she went off to college, so I didn't mind spending more time in Bahrain. Few other sailors would make that same statement, but it gave me several advancement options for my career. I could do as much or as little as I wanted with all the spare time.

I began taking online courses at my old community college to finish my associate degree. Imagine that. Many assume that people who join the military dislike school or are too stupid for higher education, but that's simply not the case. Over the next year or so, I would finish my associate degree while the U.S. Navy paid for it. I never had to pay one dime and was actually reimbursed for the student loans that resulted from my previous schooling.

During this time, I kept in contact with my MA friends but made sure to avoid situations that could get me in trouble. I didn't want to get involved an alcohol-related incident or anything else out in town that could be deemed detrimental to the navy's or the United States' image. While serving in Bahrain, a group of sailors whom I'd actually gone through the academy with stole a Shia flag from some local's house while drunk. If that wasn't bad enough, a certain group of sailors decided to smear their own feces all over the barracks' walls while drunk. Why somebody would do this, I have no idea, but it's the type of behavior that I wanted to avoid. There's a saying that the five people you surround yourself with are the people that you become. Instinctively, I made sure I was in the right company.

In April of 2004, the navy sent me to Lackland Air Force Base in San Antonio for twelve weeks of training dogs—or rather, dogs training me. The navy normally required those who'd achieved a higher rank to attend the dog school. I wasn't the first seaman, but I was one of the earlier ones they allowed to attend.

I hated Lackland when I first arrived. I wore a desert camouflage uniform as a navy seaman serving overseas, and everybody else wore the typical green Battle Dress Uniforms (BDUs) worn stateside. A random MA told me that I couldn't wear the uniforms that I had brought with me because they were from my Bahrain command, but I had never had any other uniforms in the navy. The command master chief (CMC) quickly corrected that situation, and I no longer had to deal with the constant questioning due to wearing an overseas uniform. Whenever the CMC says you're good, everything usually has a way of working itself out. It did help that he understood the duty station of Bahrain and that he had just been over there. On top of that, he knew that I was young and that the only uniforms I'd been issued were the janitor-looking uniform from boot camp and the uniforms from Bahrain. I dealt with a lot of crap—mainly from those who had no reason to mess with me—because most of my peers at the school outranked me. I stayed respectful, controlled my military bearing, and kept a squared away uniform. The military sometimes requires you to endure some petty stuff. The start of my twelve weeks at Military Working Dog Handler Course began with patrol school. That consisted of dogs basically dragging us around the damn compound because none of them had any obedience and the instructors all knew we had no skills when it came to handling dogs. In particular, every morning began with the dogs hauling us around Shit Hill. We walked the dogs on leash around in a circle on a hill as the dogs dragged our asses around looking for a place to crap. We did this first thing because we wanted to avoid them crapping inside a scenario, which would throw off all the rest of the dogs and delay training. Whether we were conducting a building search, an open area search, or some other type of patrol work, we didn't want that happening.

In general, the military used a variety of dog breeds for the work we did—anywhere from a highly driven Malinois to a Labrador retriever. That differed from the dogs at ███████████████████████████████ ██████████████████████████████. We needed them to do things that we'd never ask of other types of dogs in the military.

████████ primarily used Belgian Malinois and Dutch shepherds. Their body composition and natural drive gave them the tools needed for that special type of work. I'm not suggesting that a German shepherd doesn't have a melon or the right kind of drive, but a typical Belgian Malinois and Dutch shepherd has so much drive that it would propel them to do the work we needed them to do. I have seen a Belgian Malinois get shot and remain in the fight. I've also seen my personal dog, Digo, get blown up and tossed across a courtyard and continue to try to bite random people because he was so pissed off. I find these dogs' pain tolerance incredible. They'll pretty much go dead tired until they're actually dead. We often have to simply protect them from themselves.

We had to monitor how much we worked them and the amount of water they consumed afterwards. Too much water or food intake after a heavy workout or training session could result in serious harm for the dog.

At ████████ the majority of the canines were males, but if a female had something special that made them stand out above all other female dogs (and even some male dogs) that we tested, we'd certainly use them. I would say that most of our dogs had a unique aspect to them that stood out during testing, which led us to select them. We weren't going for quantity but rather quality. We sent a huge number of dogs back from ████████ The attrition rate for selecting dogs mirrored other special military units. We had no room for mediocrity, and we definitely didn't have time to figure out whether the animal needed more time to get combat ready. We needed good dogs that could do the work.

At the handlers course back in San Antonio, they didn't even give us a dog to start off with. We began with ammo cans just as I had in Bahrain, and once again, I stood there wondering when the hell I'd get a dog. You can only correct or reward an ammo can so much before you actually think the ammo can has some type of damn feelings. I felt like an idiot just as I had in Bahrain. But now, I had several classmates alongside me, and we could feel like idiots together. I praised the hell out of that ammo can because I wanted everybody to know that I wanted to become a dog handler. So, we spent our first week with ammo cans, but that would soon change.

Every morning, we'd show up for PT on the concrete pad out front, and from there, we would move into our training for the day. They'd let us clean up; then, we'd be right back out training. I don't remember its name, but they assigned me this hard-ass shepherd for my first dog. It didn't know how to release a bite and wasn't able to follow my commands other than to sit.

We spent the first week on obedience training for dogs that had none, so things didn't exactly go well. During that week, we focused on basic commands like sit, down, heel, here, or come. We had to say the commands loudly, which sounded crazy. When I train dogs now, I barely even raise my voice when giving commands. Most of the time, people can't even hear me. It's not necessary to use a loud or forceful voice to get a dog to do anything, but for training purposes, we were instructed to use loud, crisp, and clear commands.

At ███████████, however, most if not all of our dogs were imported from overseas, and we relied on the language of the country we were buying them from. Following are some examples of commands. We commonly used Dutch, the language many of the dogs already knew.

> *Zit* – Sit
>
> *Volg* – Heel
>
> *Aff* – Down
>
> *Hier* – Here
>
> *Apport* – Bring
>
> *Stellen* – Bite
>
> *Voruit* – Go out
>
> *Braaf* – Good boy
>
> *Foei* – No
>
> *Zook* – Article search/search for explosives
>
> *Revieren* – Go out and search for bad guy

I enjoyed my time at the school, but it did not come without issues. One particular staff sergeant in charge of my course did everything to try to break me. I don't know why he had it out for me, but he did. The Marine Corps taught hand-to-hand combat and had a program in Bahrain where we could train with them and earn different colored belts. He would turn the Marines against me because we were all young and fresh in the military. He thought it was cool to try to get the Marines to choke me out, but neither the Marines nor I fell for his bullshit.

Once again, I learned what kind of leader I wanted to be. It definitely wasn't what that guy displayed. In life, we all have to deal with people who abuse their authority, and we have to pick and choose our battles. We can't let them hurt our feelings, and we must try to find what parts of the leadership are effective. We all learn in different ways, and a good leader really needs to evaluate his people and recognize how they work and how they learn. That's one thing I discovered through my experiences with this staff sergeant and other leaders throughout my career.

From obedience, we moved on to basic bite work. Now, the words "halt, halt, halt," or "I will release my dog," are ingrained into my skull. We had to say it like that every single time we released our dog. The instructors preferred we get our dog to release or come off a decoy, but sometimes, we had to choke the dog off because they wouldn't obey. They didn't fail us for that because they knew we worked with dogs that would never make it in the fleet.

From there, we shifted to building searches, which involved working our dog to search a building on a long line. To this day, I have no idea why we used long lines in the military when we had electronic collars available to guide and control the dogs at a distance. I have found electronic collars a valuable tool for training. I know some will think it's mean, but I've seen dogs do amazing things using the e-collar, while some average pet owners have euthanized their dogs because they couldn't get control of them.

During open area searches, we got covered in ticks and chiggers because the dogs would start at point A in a field, and a decoy would be all the way out in the field hiding. We had to mark when the dog gave us a change of behavior. That is when it began searching and threw up their nose or did something special with their body language to tell us they were on a person. I really enjoyed that part of the training except for the chiggers. It came to a point where I had my belt so tight that the chiggers would stop at the beltline, but by that time, they covered my legs and left tiny little bumps a day later. One time, they got so bad I had to make a trip to the hospital and then get put in sick quarters for three days because I could barely move.

I graduated from block one of the six-week course for the Military Working Dog Handler Course and then moved on to block two—all scent detection. The dogs had no obedience for that. I remember a lab pulling me down the road every single day. My hand ended up purple by the time we arrived. We weren't allowed to choke or correct any of those dogs, so we were pretty much at their mercy. Every day, they dragged me from the trailer to the building where we would do the training scenario.

A lot of those dogs would have false response issues, meaning they would sit on random spots, telling us they found a training aid where there wasn't one. Most of the time, they did this so they could just receive their damn toy. I give them credit though. When you have a human on the end of the line who doesn't yet know his head from his ass when it comes to training a dog... Well, I would react the same way in that situation. As a result, I had to figure out when the dog gave a correct response versus when they were bluffing me only to get their reward.

We had to take the standard military multiple-choice tests where two answers were wrong, one was partially right and partially wrong (the kind that screws you), and one answer was completely right. These tests focused on concepts such as operant conditioning and classical conditioning. To be honest, the tricky wording in the tests confused the hell out of me. Later in life, I met Bart Bellon, who made this much easier to understand because he had a way of explaining all of that in clearer terms. He's pretty much a genius when it comes to dog behavior and training.

Detection consisted of searching things like buildings, vehicles, planes, and parcels. For six weeks, we would continue block two counting down the days. Once we figured out detection, which only took about a week and a half to two weeks, we simply wanted to be done. I found detection, by far, the most boring of the two blocks in training. It seemed like one of those things in the military where everything needed to be dragged out over a period of weeks.

Everything became redundant, but that is kind of the military's way of making sure that those a little behind have the opportunity to learn what they need to know. I believe that many schools in the military are set up for everyone to pass. It may take the lowest person longer to get it, but they eventually pass and move on. For example, we had one guy in boot camp who just couldn't get it. He was rolled back and eventually graduated. There's always some job in the military for those wanting to serve.

Regarding dog handling and training though, I now have a newfound appreciation for the length of time that they kept us at school. Nothing in dog training replaces repetition and experience. There's no book you can simply read and expect to learn it all. Books are important, but what's more important in my opinion is physically putting eyes and hands on multiple dogs to be able to read what it is they're doing. Personally, I want to see who taught you as a trainer and who apprenticed under you. Going to these civilian schools is great, but training one to three dogs like I did when I went to the Tom Rose School for Professional Dog Trainers after the military did not make me a great trainer, even though my dogs looked great at school.

———————

I arrived back in Bahrain for another year of service, eager to receive my first dog. It was at this point that I was assigned a dog named Bren—an all-black German shepherd. Initially, it disappointed me that he couldn't do patrol work, meaning that he could not do the bite work because his hips were not strong enough. I couldn't even train bite work with him just for the fun of it. However, Bren had previously been trained for explosives work. As my first military working dog, he was the best thing that could happen to me at the time. He knew how to do everything on his own, and I was merely an extension of him, connected by the leash. I think if he could, he would have done it all independently.

I was eager to start working with Bren on explosives work. We would pull out sodium chlorate and potassium chlorate and run training sessions all throughout the base. I love training, and even though he wasn't a patrol dog, I still had a wonderful time. I would cruise around the base in my minivan with a dog crate, bumpin' Mike Jones, Paul Wall, and anything that chopped and screwed. If you don't know what kind of music that is, you probably won't like it, but at the time, I enjoyed the hell out of it. Around I cruised, a 130-pound white boy, jamming to that music in my minivan. I think people at the time probably thought it was a joke, but for me, it made all the difference in my day.

I was soon placed on the night shift. That allowed me to do whatever I wanted and train wherever I wanted without having a bunch of people interfere. It offered me the opportunity to bond with my dog. As a single man with my mom and sister so far way, I simply looked forward to working with the dog, and that made my life complete again.

Bren and I worked toward our certification so that we could be called upon to sweep vehicles, boats, packages, and planes. To accomplish that, we would have to find a variety of explosives like TNT, time fuses, detonation cords, potassium chlorate, and sodium chlorate. The individuals testing us would hide those substances in a warehouse, vehicle lot, or some other area, and the base security officer would observe the certification. Our goal was to find every bit of the substance without false responses. We had to observe caution with training aids because a blowing wind could throw the dog's nose off. Odor can pool up in a certain area and present a stronger scent than when the dog is directly on the training aid. In training, we used varying amounts of those training aids but had to use caution in overusing them. Fortunately, Bren and I passed his certification to be eligible to inspect vehicles and/or any other potential places a threat could exist.

That certification also meant we could deploy. I use that word cautiously—it meant nothing more than traveling to another country, enjoying my time, and making some good money, but it was simply a temporary duty assignment. When I went to Bahrain, I assumed I'd end up in Iraq, but at the time, that couldn't be farther from the truth. The U.S. Navy sent me to the United Arab Emirates (UAE), specifically Fujairah and Dubai. They put us up in a little villa with assigned drivers that took us to work and then back to the house.

In Fujairah, I found myself feeling pretty bored. I ended up saving a lot of money, so in hindsight, I should have kept going there and bulking up my savings. In Dubai, we were taken back and forth to the port to inspect vehicles. On our off time, we explored the city, which seemed to reflect Western culture. I'd ski and shop in the malls, so I don't recall saving much money in that location. I made 130 dollars a day in per diem, which seemed like a lot. It's not, in reality, but a nice extra over the normal military pay.

We all wanted that Dubai duty but had to rotate every three weeks between twenty or so handlers for three spots, so we had some healthy competition. Like everything I did in patrols and at the kennel, I kept my nose down and worked hard so I could go a bunch of times. Later, in 2009, some leaders investigated my career, wondering why I received some favored assignments while only an E-3 or E-4 paygrade. Some assumed I belonged to a good ol' boy club, but I honestly worked my ass off for what I wanted. As a business owner today, I reward the people I know I can trust, and that allows me to focus on what I want to do with the knowledge that they have things covered. Back then, I think I gave the kennel master great trust that I would do the right thing and not cause any problems while working by myself. That sort of peace of mind means you can continue to reward the people you can count on.

Now, it may seem like I'm a poster boy for the good sailor, and that I didn't do anything wrong over in Bahrain, but I will tell you that is far from the truth. People are not perfect, and I by no means consider myself to have been.

I remember a time when I had Bren in the back of a van with another dog named Tony. Tony looked like a dog version of Oscar the grouch. He was ugly as hell but definitely had a great personality! Tony hated Bren, and the feeling was mutual. Well, guess what happened with an unlatched crate for Tony and Bren? A dog fight. My dumb ass had forgotten to latch the crate door, and the handler for Tony thought I had taken my dog out of the van. In fact, I had just run in real quick to grab some equipment so I could fill up.

I think the open crate door shocked Bren, but when he launched at it and found himself liberated, he proceeded to get into it with Tony. Too late to prevent the fight from happening, I rushed over and stuck my arm right between both dogs with a fist to break up the fight, which was probably the dumbest thing to do. Sure enough, I got bit. It was my first dog bite in the military and quite a nasty one. I could see the vein in my wrist and my main artery pumping. At least the dogs sustained no injuries.

Another time, I thought it would be cute to kiss a dog on its face. That was no ordinary dog—one that I happened to work with on deployment in the UAE. We found it funny that the dog would growl a little bit whenever anyone got close to it, but we could pet him while he lay in his bed. He belonged to another handler in Fujairah who bet me I couldn't kiss the dog. What do you think I did? I tried to kiss the dog. That resulted in a bite to the face, a torn tear duct, and me looking like an utter idiot because I had done something stupid. We didn't tell anyone that we had a bet—I didn't want that handler to get in trouble. I planned to take full responsibility, even if that meant losing my handler privileges. After that incident, I realized that I needed to tighten up, and from that moment forward, I put my nose to the pavement and didn't look back. Life could always get worse, and I think knowing that helped me move forward!

Over the course of two and a half years in Bahrain, I worked with two other dogs. Shecker, an all-black flat-coated retriever, did not like having his ass petted, and people liked to tease him. As I'm writing this, I have a better appreciation for the stories people tell me when they bring their dogs for training. Often, I ask myself why the hell do people do these things? People do stupid stuff. No one is exempt from making a stupid choice, and that includes me. Touching Shecker's booty was an unwise move, but that's how some in the military roll. Shecker had only trained as a bomb dog, so they relegated me to sweeping vehicles. I'd get another chance with a single-purpose dog, and duty with Shecker kept me engaged and returning to Dubai.

After Shecker, I worked with a pretty cool black-faced Belgian Malinois named Leo. I taught him how to sit pretty, meaning he sat up on his back legs with his front paws in the air kind of like a meerkat. At this point, I finally got to do what I really wanted to—bite work. When I picked him up at the tarmac, I tried to talk my kennel master into letting me work that dog. Little did I know he was already going to pair me with Leo because of the trust he had in me. That meant a lot considering the stupid shit I had done.

The dog came from Lackland and was pretty green but had a ton of potential. He could also be temperamental when it came to being picked up and things like that. In fact, that's why I now tell new puppy owners to really handle their pups so the first and only times are not at the veterinarian's office. I really loved that dog though because he taught me so much. All the dogs taught me a lot of lessons, but with Leo, I really learned how to train and do my job while he was learning as well. That synergy helped us troubleshoot and determine how to move forward with excellence.

Watching Leo do bite work was the coolest. He was a sixty-pound fur missile and a complete badass. I could teach that dog a nasty bark and hold, which required him to sit in front of the decoy and just bark. I gave the command, and he moved to the decoy, barked, and held. Eventually, we wanted to take it up a step, so the bark and hold turned into a bark, jump in the face, and snap. In hindsight, that probably wasn't a smart idea, but it seemed cool at the time.

As my time in Bahrain neared the end, so did my time in the military—or so I thought. I had a choice of orders because I had spent so much time in Bahrain. They could leave me overseas, but the navy would likely send me back to the States. Navy detailers in some office in Tennessee held the fate of sailors and officers in the palm of their hand. With a few keystrokes, they could send me to sunny Florida or the Northwest like Washington state where it rains. I'm not knocking either option, but I did my best to make friends and use my connections to gain an assignment where I wanted to serve next. I certainly had locations that I preferred, but for my career, they suggested I work at a smaller kennel where I'd have more responsibilities.

In Bahrain, I did have a lot of responsibilities, but to hold some of those key leadership positions, such as taking charge of the explosive program for our kennel, I had to be a little higher up in rank. Honestly, there were a lot more sailors that were higher ranking than me, and it was important for them to have those positions so they could compete against other sailors for rank. Extra duties or responsibilities went a long way toward being promoted.

Regardless, I wanted to make a move but didn't know where to go. Others advised me that south Texas was a great place to serve and could add to my specialty for career advancement. Many elements of my life today are a result of that choice to go to Kingsville, Texas. I had listed a couple of other places but ultimately put that location as my number one choice because I'd have the opportunity to apply to state and local agencies for a police officer position if I left the navy. Essentially, I'd have a leg up on other applicants by taking that path. So off to Kingsville I went.

Bahrain was hot, but I don't think anything could have prepared me for the heat and humidity of south Texas. I didn't know much about Kingsville, but I knew that I could make the short drive to Corpus Christi for the coast with the possibility of fishing among other activities. I didn't realize there wouldn't be anything to do in Kingsville. At the time, in 2007, they had the base, Walmart, and of course several Mexican restaurants. Not much else at all. I could understand how many would get in trouble for underage drinking and the other dumb things young people do simply because of boredom.

I had become accustomed to living out in town in Bahrain as an E-4. I had all my household goods and everything that I had accumulated with me when I moved back to the United States. However, the navy only allowed E-5s and above to live off base in the United States. That relegated me to the black-mold-filled barracks full of fuckery and debauchery. I did not take that news very well because I had all this stuff, was pretty independent, and was used to living on my own. I certainly didn't like being treated like a child after spending three years in one of the navy's top dog kennels. Everything I'd achieved did not matter. They only cared about rank without considering anything else. So I was stuck in the barracks, but that would soon work itself out.

Like most people (especially military people), the first thing I did after returning from overseas and making a lot of money there was buy a brand-new truck: a Ford F-150 outfitted with the latest state-of-the-art sound equipment and other bells and whistles. I also purchased a big-screen projection TV for my little ass barracks room. I figured that if I had to live there, I'd make the best of it, and there were no rules on how big of a TV I could have.

We had some dirty people in the U.S. Navy that chose to do drugs and other illegal stuff, so my barracks room was subject to random inspection. However, I made it a pain in the ass for them to come in and look at my barracks room. I had a lock around my drawers that I had to come and physically unlock. Plus, I had my bed pushed in front of the closet, and I had to move it for them whenever they came in to inspect. Sure, a pain in the ass for me, but more of a pain in the ass for them because they'd have to call for me to leave work. I had nothing to hide, but if they insisted on treating me like a child, then I would make sure I did everything possible to make their life suck while inspecting the barracks.

When I checked into the base and got all my qualifications so I could arm up, I met my first NAS Kingsville dog, Kitt, an older dog with cataracts that could really only do detection. I had a good time with him because he not only obeyed but seemed really smart, so I never had to worry about him screwing up on missing any odor or training aids. That work was too easy, and I needed an out.

While Kingsville led to me working with the SEAL teams, it's also where I met my future wife, Erica. I have to admit that I had noticed her a few times, but I don't know when the first time was. It happened either in the barracks or in the security department. She worked as an air traffic controller, and once a month, they had to come over and do Auxiliary Security Force (ASF) assignments. I thought that she was so beautiful and loved that she didn't give a damn about what anybody else thought. Her cool and her confidence impressed me.

I remember seeing her in the security building back in 2006, as she had to do ASF. Luckily for me, we were both stuck in the barracks. I managed to work my way into a conversation with her one day with the help of one of her coworkers.

Several guys told me that she didn't date and especially not navy guys. I thought *great* but still wanted to take a chance to ask her out and see if anything resulted from that. When we started dating, she took a lot of flak because she had changed her mind when it came to me. The first thing Erica invited me out for was a toga party in the barracks. We had a few drinks, we kicked it off, and the rest is history.

Our first few dates didn't come without some ups and downs. Erica quickly taught me several ways to enjoy Kingsville, Texas, including all the little-known spots and the best places to dance and have a drink. I learned that Erica didn't mind going out to party, and I had been invited to this shindig out in town by a military couple that had rented out a place for a house party. The crowd got so damn big that both the local police and base police showed up.

As you can imagine, being the new guy and getting caught up in this after only two weeks on base didn't look good. Reluctantly, I showed my ID, and let's just say I received a stern talking-to the next day. I wasn't intoxicated or anything like that, but the simple fact that I attended this party at all showed poor judgment. That wasn't the only lesson I learned. One of other "shining" moments involved learning how to drink Texas Tea. To my surprise, a cool $10 bought you a little jug of tea that was simply plain old alcohol. Needless to say, I didn't handle my Texas Tea too well.

I believed from the moment I saw Erica that she was the one. I don't think I ever really believed in that up until then because of all the stuff I had gone through with previous relationships, but I strongly believed there was something special about her. I also believed that God had put her in my path because of the road I'd soon travel in life. I'd lean on Erica's strength more than once. I only found a couple good things to come out of Kingsville, and she was one of them.

Over the next couple of months, Erica and I continued to date, and it was the happiest that I had been in a very long time. I felt like I was now going through life with someone else—I wasn't just alone.

Ultimately, though, I felt some emptiness. I experienced a sense of purposelessness in my job since I felt I could do so much more. In an attempt to fill this void, I began riding along with Texas State Patrol. I enjoyed spending time with those guys and gals so much that I ended up applying for the Texas State Patrol. After passing the test and the physical, I realized I would soon have to make a choice because my end of service date was approaching. At that point, I was scheduled to get out in August of 2007, and while I enjoyed working as a military dog handler in general, I didn't find fulfillment in the tasks, such as sweeping vehicles at a gate and training all day, required at Kingsville.

I needed to do something else, and I'd soon have to test my relationship with Erica. Keep in mind, I had tested a past relationship when I joined the U.S. Navy and then again when I left for Bahrain. Neither time had worked out, and in fact, it had sucked. It would soon suck again. If I waited around in Kingsville, I didn't have any assurance that the Texas State Patrol would keep me near Erica.

One day, while I while driving around, a good friend and fellow dog handler called me. The SEAL teams had selected him for some dog training and handling. I had met him in Bahrain, and he had been a good mentor to me while we were there. Because we had no family over there, the handlers had indeed become my family. I had no intention of becoming a SEAL but thought working with them would be cool. Once he told me all the things he'd done with the SEALs, I knew that I wanted that as well. I wanted to do more complex things with the dogs, and I also wanted to deploy. I could do that with the SEALs.

At first, this friend didn't tell me why he had called, but he finally revealed that the SEAL teams needed more dog handlers. Furthermore, he said he'd vouch for me and my skills as a dog handler. While those attributes didn't carry much weight in Kingsville, they mattered to him and to those he recommended my services to. He made no guarantees but stated that I could have the opportunity to test and screen for a spot. What he described didn't sound easy, but I honestly didn't care because I wanted out of Kingsville. I did not know what that meant for me and Erica, but I thought that if God wanted it to be, it would. I told my friend I wanted that chance, so SEAL Team ■ would soon contact my command and ask for permission to allow me to go up and screen for the position.

I traveled to the Norfolk, Virginia, area and was taken to a base compound in Virginia Beach. I'm not at liberty to share more details about that location but can say that I found it one awesome place. The amount of security SEAL Team ■ took me through was truly shocking. They drove me through a series of gates and guided me through the signing of paperwork.

I ultimately made my way toward the back to the kennel. While there, I met several people. I had no idea who they were, and they didn't know me, but I did my best to set a good example of my capabilities. I really didn't have to try because I'm no pretender. I planned to show them what I could do and what they'd get. I've always found just being genuine about who I am is way better than going out of my way to simply impress.

I helped with kennel cleaning, training, and anything else I could. We'd been brought in a week before so they could see how we would do around the dogs before the regular command screening. Of course, I had to endure a bunch of that administrative stuff that technically did mean something, but what mattered most was whether I could handle the dogs and whether they could trust me to run alongside them.

One of my more interesting memories there involved an old master chief named Jack. He had served at "the command" for a long time and led the dog kennel. I remember the day he took me out on a run and said he would take me to the obstacle course that the SEALs had made. I didn't really think anything of it. As a twenty-one-year-old running with a guy who must have been fifty, I thought that I would have no problem. He was a lean machine and probably no more than five-foot-seven. Man, was I in for a world of hurt. He ran me five miles to the obstacle course, ran the course, and then ran back. He absolutely punished me, and then he had me do some pullups after my arms were already dead. I had never used those types of muscles in my body, regardless of how much I had worked out in the past. That guy could outrun me and outdo me on any of those physical challenges. After I finished the pullups, he told me, "You really should be able to more than that." Nothing better than eating a piece of humble pie. That experience showed me that I had entered a whole new world where the standard for Navy SEAL fitness far outweighed anything I had done before. Age didn't matter.

My time there would come to an end after two weeks, and I had the hardest time being away from Erica. I knew that if I was selected, we'd endure long separations. Could we survive that? At that age, I only thought if I chose someone over that opportunity, I would look back and regret it. Little did I know that Erica had the determination to stay with me, and I had the determination to stay with her.

While at the command, I went through a series of psychological and physical tests, including an interview on why I should be a part of their team. After I finished the screening, I headed back to Kingsville to await the verdict. Would I get in? I had decided that if they didn't select me, I would probably leave the military. After seeing what they did with their dogs, I realized not being part of that would leave me nothing else to do in the military. I couldn't go unfulfilled, so I would stop working with dogs altogether. I would simply look for the next bigger thing to do, whether in the navy or as a police officer.

Soon after, I got the call. They had accepted me into their program! Ultimately, it had come down to a vote among all the people who worked in the dog kennel to allow me in or out. I believe to this day no one voted me out, but I think some questioned how young I was. An underdog. I was only twenty-one at the time, while the average operator was thirty years old, give or take a couple of years.

The only remaining hurdle was for my base commanding officer and my security officer to release me from their command. I had an amazing kennel supervisor named Jill. She could have said, "No, we need you here," but instead, she gave her recommendation. I believe that without her doing that, it wouldn't have happened. I found her to be a hardheaded, no-bull-shit-taking female, and I respected her because of that. I am so grateful to her as well as my security officer and my commanding officer for letting me pursue that opportunity.

I had arrived in Kingsville in June of 2006, not knowing what direction I'd head after the military. In February of 2007, I left for SEAL Team ██.

Benny, Erica, Jacob, and Emma attending the chief petty officer pinning in 2012.

Benny with Brando after trenching through waist-deep water while chasing a squirter on an objective in 2011.

Benny with Brando on a target objective during a mission in 2011.

Benny with Brando and SEAL Team ▮ after a mission in 2011.

Benny and Tigo after completing an assault of a target objective in Afghanistan.

Benny and Leo patrolling the pier at NSA Bahrain in 2005.

Returning with Tigo to base on a CH-47 Chinook helicopter after a mission in Afghanistan.

Benny and Twan (the angry Korean) during Benny's retirement ceremony in 2013.

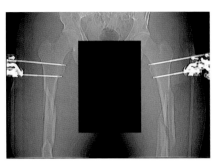

The extent of Benny's femur fractures from an IED explosion in 2008.

Benny and Rex on a target objective in 2010.

Benny and Jet (John Douangdara) taking out time from training to play on a local abandoned playground.

Benny and Rex on a target objective in 2010.

Benny with Digo and SEAL Team ■ after a mission in 2008.

Benny and Brando prior to leaving on a target objective in 2011.

Benny and Digo practicing climbing over walls in preparation for deployment to Iraq.

Benny and Brando prior to leaving on a target objective in 2011.

Benny and Brando while on a target objective in 2011.

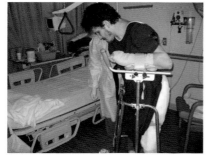

Benny learning to walk again after doctors fixed two shattered femurs and his wrist.

Digo after returning to base from an objective in 2008.

Benny in a wheelchair just three weeks after he was blown up holding three-week-old baby Jacob.

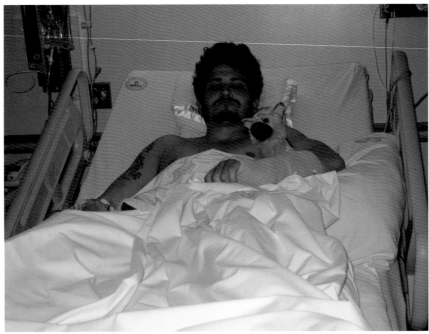

Benny lying in the hospital in Bethesda, Maryland, after being blown up by an HBIED.

Benny and Digo after a mission in 2008 where Digo found an insurgent with a fully loaded PKM. The duo ultimately saved lives that night.

Benny and his kids during the U.S. Navy chief pinning ceremony in 2012.

Benny and Digo being awarded the Purple Heart medal for being critically injured during a combat mission in Iraq.

Benny and Digo receiving the Purple Heart medal.

Benny and Digo riding in a Humvee to a daytime target objective in Iraq in 2008.

Benny and his kids after his U.S. Navy chief pinning ceremony in 2012 on board Joint Expeditionary Base Little Creek-Fort Story.

Benny and his kids volunteering to lay wreaths for fallen service members.

Benny and Erica Hutchins attending the Navy Ball together at Naval Air Station Kingsville in 2007.

Military working dog Leo.

CHAPTER 6
MEETING THE SEALS

Throughout this work, I've consistently referenced the unit I conducted the most missions with as SEAL Team ██. That's the name the public knows, the name used in media sources, and the name readily available on the average internet search engine. ████████████████████████ ██ ██ ████████████████████████████████ SEAL means Sea, Air, and Land. ████████████████████████████████████ ████████████████████ Of course, any of their missions that make the news will reference something like a SEAL team out of Virginia Beach, Virginia. ████████████████████████████████ ██ ████████████████████████████

Whichever name someone might use, they all fall under Naval Special Warfare Command, whether they're the guys who deploy out of a submarine, parachute from the sky, or ride in on a helicopter. All the SEAL teams have a foundation from past irregular warfare units. For example, the

Underwater Demolition Teams (UDTs) conducted underwater missions, such as intelligence gathering prior to an invasion, in World War II. The team tasked with counterterrorism, seeking out high-value targets, hostage rescue, and various direct-action missions is typically SEAL Team ██, a ████████ with an extremely demanding selection process ██████████. The dogs that work with them also face a demanding selection process.

██ ████████████████████████████ Without going in depth on specific numbers, SEAL teams are made up of many complex departments, such as squadrons, troops, and platoons. They also have several support squadrons that provide unique skills like dog handling. My particular squadron had a couple of troops that broke down into various teams. Typically, each team had a particular task on each target mission. One team might provide security while another one conducted the main assault on the target. If we had any follow-on targets, they'd assign another team for that. Snipers usually had overwatch, whether on the walls or on other buildings or wherever they found an advantageous position.

I never experienced the stringent selection process that the SEALs go through but have heard those who endured the process considered it more difficult (and more secretive) than BUD/S, the initial selection process to become a SEAL. I do know that the selection process ensures they quickly weed out anyone who shouldn't join them so those who remain are the right ones.

For the first few months, I felt as though I were drinking water through a fire hose. During that time, I went through a number of mental and physical tests. The first day that I checked on board, I checked off all the admin boxes one does when joining a new command. The U.S. Navy loves its paperwork, and security clearance alone took significant time due to the top-secret nature of that unit. They outfitted me with all the gear I'd need for the Direct Support Course but didn't immediately assign me a dog. They had me on different tasks, and I'd work out and PT as much as possible before beginning the course.

The Direct Support Course provided basic training for anyone who would do on-target missions with the Navy SEALs. A couple of retired Navy SEALs or a SEAL at the command that needed the spot taught the course. Due to my youthfulness—I was just twenty-one years old—they definitely held me to a higher standard than anybody else. Or at least I felt that way. The typical age was twenty-eight to thirty-eight. I could be off a bit, but my peers definitely had more time than me in the navy. On top of that, I was a dog handler—one of only a few non-SEALs that would go on target, and one of only a couple that would go to the door.

One of the very first tests they had us do involved pullups, a three-mile run, and a swim, all within a required timeframe. I actually think they gave us the BUD/S entry test. We had to pass or come awfully close to stay there. The run came pretty easy for me. I weighed 140 pounds soaking wet and could do the pushups as well. I only passed the pullups by a couple because I had never done them before. As a first-timer, I supposed I shouldn't have expected to simply go and do it perfectly. As you can probably imagine, I failed the swim in the allotted time, but I had never swum the sidestroke and had no idea how to do it efficiently. Guess who didn't just quit when the time was up? I kept going because I promised myself that quitting wasn't an option. Because we had only so much time to prepare for that course, they made few exceptions, especially for those like me that would be on target during missions as opposed to back at a camp.

Over the course of eight weeks, we had multiple types of medical screenings, and they instructed us on room clearing, combat clearance, land navigation, and over the beach (OTB) training as well as other things. In addition, we learned communications and had medical training. Essentially, they seemed to focus on combat clearance and making sure we could handle a gun.

I appreciated the whole block of medical training we received. That crap came in handy during my first deployment for obvious reasons. They issued us a blowout kit and educated us on all its contents and their uses—anything from how to apply a tourniquet to how to treat an airway blockage. I found applying a tourniquet surprisingly eye-opening. Better too tight than not tight enough.

We also engaged in the controversial use of a pig lab. They brought in pigs, put them under anesthesia, and put them through any injury that might happen to a human on the battlefield. Unfortunately, war demands that type of necessary training. We had to do everything we could to keep them alive with that blowout kit. Gunshot wounds, stabbings, explosions, and anything else you can think of. Anything that could happen to us happened to those pigs. I am not trying to justify the injuring or killing of a helpless animal, but there are far worse things happening in our world for the "greater good of science." Veterinarians would later euthanize them. Despite the controversial nature of this practice, I can certainly say in retrospect that this helped us when it came time while we were overseas on deployment.

If you're still pissed that happened, please feel free to hit up the politicians that sent us. I'm still pissed that they sent us to only give Afghanistan back to our enemies, the Taliban. Another topic for another time.

For land navigation, we received a compass and a handy Garmin GPS. I wish I could say I found that course exciting, but when they dumped our asses out at Fort Pickett in Virginia in hot-ass barracks, the most exciting thing I experienced was probably taking a little mirror, spreading my butt cheeks, and looking for ticks. Good times. The number of ticks I found on me was ludicrous, to say the least. Anyway, we set out in the woods to find a set of markers, and the goal for each was to avoid coming in last. Luckily, someone in my group had the foresight to obtain the GPS coordinates. So we made our way through the woods, looking for those points and hoping that none of the instructors picked up on what we were doing.

On one of the nights, we had some free time, and while everyone else slept, we took it upon ourselves to explore whatever part of Richmond, Virginia, would be happy to serve us its finest spirits. We didn't find the finest, but we did manage to visit several establishments and consume copious amounts of alcohol. Knowing full well that a hangover the next day would screw us, we continued through the night.

Our designated driver did his duty and kindly brought us back just one hour before we had to wake up and take on the day. Little did I know that the instructors had planned for anything but a relaxing day in the woods. Rather, they had us doing iterations on the mock village—basically a make-shift site to practice house clearing or house runs through various parts of the made-up village. Enduring the unbearable heat and still drunk, I proceeded to suffer the rest of the day. Not only was it hot and miserable, but one of the SEAL instructors caught on to what had occurred overnight and proceeded to punish us with "extra training." You'd think we would've learned our lesson, but there were several times I went out when I probably should've just stayed in.

The next evolution we experienced during the Direct Support Course was OTBs. Basically, they dropped us off from a boat about two hundred meters or less away from the shoreline, and we began a long swim with everything but the kitchen sink. I found it the single most terrifying thing I had ever done while simultaneously considering it the most awesome thing. I simply kept asking myself, *Am I going to die today?* Well, I began to sink and wondered about my dry suit and whether that thing actually even worked. The suit was made of rubber dish plastic material and basically formed a seal around my neck. As I took on water, I quickly realized the seal around my neck wasn't so sealed. So I fixed it promptly and began to just float. As a poor swimmer, I certainly didn't love that part. Little did I know that I'd later have to do that with a dog.

At the time, I thought that we'd never do that crazy stuff with a dog, but it turns out that team had no issue with doing a lot of crazy stuff. They took us out in a high-speed assault craft (HSAC) or a Zodiac and dropped us off for the long swim back to the beach. Sounds easy enough, right? I wasn't much of a swimmer and also had a gun and other equipment to manage. I'm not saying I wasn't up for the challenge, but it did pose quite a test. Putting on fins in the water gave me some difficulty, but removing them before reaching the shore, and not too early, was a much bigger challenge. If you waited too long, to the point when the fins touched the sand, the weight and force of the water made that an even more difficult experience because I couldn't walk, and the waves tossed me around. I learned to use the suit and float at the right time to make it safely to shore. I also learned how to access weapons and other items in my OTB bag at just the right time.

I realize, to you, that may seem boring and maybe not too tough, but I had to master my own situation before I attempted that with a dog, a whole different experience. When dogs hit the water, they naturally splash around. Regardless of the flotation device you're using, handling them in open water takes a lot of practice.

When it came time to train with my first squadron dog, he decided to jump all over me as his personal buoy. Adding insult to injury, we had crazy waves that day, so I needed help getting him directed toward land. If a dog sees the shore, they seem to naturally want to swim that way. Since I stayed connected with a little leash, he pulled me to shore—but not until I first got stuck in the surf with my fins on. Getting tossed about by the waves in about three feet of water, I thought I'd certainly drown, but luckily, two SEALS noticed me struggling with the dog and helped me out.

After that, I really had no problems with OTB operations, but I had no desire to ever do it again unless required for an actual mission. It's one of those things—you want to say that you tried it and did it, but you don't care to ever do it again. When people ask whether getting blown up was the scariest thing I ever encountered, I say, "No, OTBs were." I found no enjoyment in that exercise. Ironic that I served in the navy but hated swimming. I'll fish and sit on the beach all day, but I'll be damned if I'd enjoy just going for a swim in the ocean. I dreaded swimming to shore with a dog and all my gear. It's why I wasn't a SEAL. I never wanted to take that pounding from the ocean. She hit me like a ton of bricks.

We had basic training with weapons as well. The cadre would take us through a series of drills, teaching us how to clear houses or just perform basic room clearance as most would call it. Essentially, they taught us just enough to not muzzle sweep anyone or get someone killed. In more basic terms, don't point your weapon at someone when clearing a room.

Combat clearance meant moving methodically through a scenario as slowly as needed to be smooth. That type of clearing typically happened when no hostages were involved and we didn't have to go balls to the wall running through a house. There's a huge difference between hostage rescue clearing of an objective and combat clearance. I'd like to think one is more about self-preservation than anything else whereas hostage rescue is about getting to the hostage and getting them out.

We began with the basic tactics and then moved on to multi-faceted facilities and training scenarios. I most enjoyed one near Memphis, Tennessee. The cadre show us a series of combat shooting drills but also put a beatdown on us. I remember them having a ladder used for ship boarding hanging from a tree, and anytime we screwed up, we had to run to the tree and climb the ladder. I lost count of how many times I had to do that.

For the most part, they trained us on a standard Colt M4 and then Sig P226. A lot of the training involved properly transitioning from a primary to a secondary weapon, reloading, and then continuing to move tactically. My fingers bled from the jamming of magazines and thousands of rounds fired. The M4 would not be my choice of weapon on later deployments, but for now, I had to learn it inside and out.

A senior chief in charge of the course, a SEAL, came up and told me he'd personally hold me more accountable than anyone else in the course, not only due to my age but because of the job I had to do. He knew I'd stand right there at the door with my dog and the operators. I needed to understand their role, certainly not hinder them, but then also move, shoot, and otherwise fight as much like them as I could. He had told me that at the beginning of the course, but I had shrugged it off due to his laidback nature in other things. But when it came to this, he changed his demeanor. Every week, we would sit down and do a debrief with the course instructor, and he'd always be the one to sit with me. He was very critical, but to this day, I am so grateful to him as well as the MA that went through the course with me. He also helped out when it came to making sure I understood exactly what I was supposed to be doing.

I didn't have much previous experience with guns other than what the navy had taught us at MA school and a little more at my first duty station. This was much different. We didn't simply go to a range to qualify and shoot 150 rounds. I found the life-and-death realistic scenarios absolutely essential.

One of my favorite drills involved diving to the bottom of the swimming pool, retrieving a round for my gun, coming back up, and shooting. If you made the shot, you were done, but if you didn't make it, you had to dive back to the bottom of that damn pool. This wasn't just qualifying at some navy installation. They would make us so damn tired that our arms felt like we'd held bricks all day instead of practiced shooting. My trigger finger felt so heavy.

I now understand why they did this. Or, rather, I understood after my first deployment why they made us do all of those extreme things. The precision required when you're on target, even when you're tired, is a matter of life and death.

The basic course was not designed to make us SEALS or do everything a SEAL could do, so there were a couple of things I didn't train in. The first one was SCUBA. It's pretty straightforward, but we didn't take dogs underwater with equipment available. In general, it's damn near impossible. Did I mention I hate swimming?

The second was skydiving. So this was tricky. Five months had passed from the time I'd finished the Direct Support Course to the time of my first deployment. I continued sucking from the fire hose of training, and now I needed to learn the dog side. Taking time to learn how to jump was not in my training plan. I would've done it, but at that time, if one of those missions overseas required a jump, they would either tandem me with another SEAL and the dog or take the SEAL dog handler. After later shattering my femurs in Iraq, I had no eagerness to learn how to skydive. It certainly wasn't high on the list. After all, I would fight like hell just to do basic stuff after I got hurt. I wanted nothing more than to just get back to doing runs in the house with the team and my dog.

I graduated, or rather passed, the Direct Support Course. Did I pass with flying colors? Probably not. I think the cadre had a few laughs at my expense watching me swim, but they saw that I was willing to put in the work, no matter my size or age. I had played the underdog again. Others had assumed I was too young, too scrawny. However, they realized I wanted to be there and would do whatever it took. To this day, it's a testament to that course that it's probably what saved me in many ways, especially the life-saving skills like the medical part. When I later lay there with two broken legs from the explosion, I may not have been able to apply a tourniquet, but I did remember where and when to take a fentanyl lollipop. In the support course, they hammered it into us to keep one in our left arm shoulder pocket for quick and easy access.

I was assigned to the ████ Squadron, one of the squadrons within the SEAL teams. By completing the Direct Support Course, it basically said that I was good enough to run with them and not dumb enough to get anybody killed. Immediately upon entering the team room, I knew that I would face some uphill challenges. The first and most obvious one was the fact that I didn't wear a Trident, the Special Warfare insignia worn on the chest of those who have completed their SEAL training. I was okay with that. I knew that I had some huge shoes to fill—those of the MAs who had gone before me.

████ Squadron was the perfect storm for me. They really accepted the dogs, especially the troop they assigned me to. I'd soon learn that most of them always wanted to use the dogs. It may have been an ego thing, but some of them likely wanted to go through the door first and were reluctant to give up that opportunity. However, over time, they learned the value of the dog going first. Those guys, highly trained professionals, loved what they did but found perfect harmony, as odd as that sounds, with what we did using the dog.

Several SEALs seemed accepting of me at first. I would say the most accepting person was Luis Souffront, an EOD guy. He would definitely become instrumental in my success. He often took the time to just break down the different IEDs that we came across but also offered tips about how to get along with the guys. Luis joined the U.S. Navy in 2000 and was highly respected by the SEALs. I'm 100 percent sure they considered him their equal. But for being so good at what he did, he was humble. There was no ego to him.

During that first time in the squadron, the other members certainly saw me as an outsider, but after getting blown up and then deciding to come back, they then viewed me as—well, not necessarily an equal, but they saw me with some level of respect. Overall, I would say I felt well received by the guys. Whether they wanted me there or not was an entirely different story. I realized that early on and accepted it. After all, I skipped all the years of serving on a platoon and attending BUD/S. The training that they had to endure to get there surely mattered, and I understood that. You could say I sort of bypassed the whole board of monopoly, collected two hundred bucks, and hit free parking several times on my way to Boardwalk.

My first team leader, Mikey, a SEAL and dog handler, seemed a little crazy in my opinion. Even so, he probably saved my life by holding me accountable and maintaining a hard edge with me. He'd chew me out when I screwed up because he knew my past and recognized that an ass chewing was how I best learned. I literally went on target with the best of the best to track down the worst of the worst. I wanted the structure, and I wanted to know how to do my job to the best of my ability.

Often, those SEALs would come down from their typical role and become a dog handler to lead the three or four dog handlers assigned to the squadron. Normally, the dog handlers were MAs, but sometimes, SEALs from other teams came to the kennel for that training. Some of them made great handlers, and I think, for the most part, the U.S. Navy chose MAs for their handling skills. They wanted the guy who best handled the dog. So we had this unique mix of SEALs and MAs handling dogs on target with the teams. Typically, a SEAL, experienced at handling dogs, served as team leader for all the dog handlers. Essentially, they would act as a liai-son between all the handlers and the squadron. Later, after I returned to deployment following my recovery, I became the very first MA to assume that role as the handler team leader.

Several times on my first deployment, Mikey spotted me looking around at the front door when I should have been focusing on the rear security as needed. The first time I did that, Mikey delivered a little bit of ass chewing because, at the end of the day, it's not necessarily what's in front of you that kills you—it's what's behind you. I believe that he also knew a little bit of my history, knew I was up for the task and that I had handled pressure in my life before. I never shied away from something extreme and always looked for a way to overcome life's hurdles. That previous life experience had, over time, built calluses that helped me fight through challenges when others, or even myself, considered me an underdog.

Though I wasn't a SEAL, I had the same gear for a typical SEAL team operator loadout. If you know anything about the SEALs in general, they are loaded out with some of the best gear. Now, take into account that I served with the SEAL teams. Imagine receiving whatever the hell you need, no matter how ridiculous it may be. Research and development is huge in that world, so refining what makes them better than the enemy always comes number one. As a non-SEAL, I had the opportunity to use such gear that wasn't necessarily given to me right away. I had to make connections with several supply guys and SEALs that would "hook us up" with some of the new gear. We called this our kit or the combination of gear we used in the field.

I had a "cage" where I would keep all my gear; it seemed like its own little tactical store. We'd receive new stuff, but sometimes, what we had already became comfortable and simply good enough. I had a cage in the squadron area, but because I spent so much time training dogs at the kennel, I often used my cage there. It just made sense.

I had Crye Precision pants and top with an Under Armour beanie to keep my head warm on the cool Iraqi winter nights. A modular integrated communications helmet protected my head. It came to me in a plain tan, so I painted some leaves on it. I wore low-cut Salomon boots that ensured solid footing, but I also found them comfortable, and I could run well in them. Much better than the extra weight of big-ass desert boots. Unlike in the movies, I wore no face paint. We weren't in the jungle and mostly went out at night, so face paint didn't make sense.

For protection against small arms fire and shrapnel, I wore a ███████ ███████ plate carrier vest. Ostensibly, it protected my chest, stomach, sides, and back from projectiles, though I had no illusions that it provided a bulletproof shield like Superman. Plates stopping rounds was more of a crapshoot. It seemed like everybody I knew who got shot either took rounds through the side where the vest provided less protection or got hit some other place on their body.

The enemy used black tip or armor-piercing rounds, and I don't think the armor would stop something like that. Nor would it prevent a 7.62mm round from an AK-47 at close range from getting through. To be honest, I think wearing armor gave me more of the ability to say I wore as much protection as I should if something happened to me. I know my wife would have been pissed if I'd been killed without it on. Trust me, though, there were times when we had long or steep hikes, so I would run with chicken plates and a harness that held just the essential things I needed on target. I did that to be lighter. Stupid, yes, but lighter.

On top of my ballistic helmet sat my NVGs. For comms (communication), I wore a Peltor headset, which looked a bit like a gaming headset with a boom microphone in front of the mouth. I had a push-to-talk connected to the radio on the left side attached to the London Bridge plate carrier. Rarely did I switch channels to talk to anybody else. Typically, I waited for instructions from the team leader or the troop chief rather than initiating conversations.

I'd also hook up a little MP3 player to my headset as most guys did. I'd always listen to music in the helicopter or vehicle en route to targets. I typically queued up some of my favorite metal or classic rap tunes that always set the mood. That amped me up. Although heading out with guys of the caliber I operated with was enough to set the mood. They were all business.

Of course, Digo had his own mood. Somewhere between relentless and psychotic. Always amped up and always in the right mood to take someone out.

Normally, I rolled with a Colt M4 carbine assault rifle 5.56mm with a suppressor, but when I slung it on my left side, the same side as my dog, the suppressor would smack the animal in the head. So, sometimes, I used an MP5 9mm submachine gun. The shorter MP5 worked better in close quarters. I just happened to go with that smaller German weapon the night of the explosion. For extra firepower, I carried a Sig Sauer 226 chambered in 9mm. To top it all off, I carried a Benchmade knife strapped to the front of my gear. It wasn't a Winkler knife—I would have to do a couple of deployments to earn that.

In a small backpack, I placed a mesh muzzle and some water for the dog, who essentially had his own kit I'd outfit him in for a mission. We both had all of the same medical supplies needed to take care of us, just in case. On my left side, I strapped my med kit, and I had the dog on my right. I always carried two, one for each of us. I placed a Fentanyl lollipop in my left shoulder pocket. I had no way of knowing would soon come in handy.

Everyone on those teams, regardless of role, nuanced their kit for personal preference. Rarely did two of us on a mission have an identical setup. For example, my gloves had the fingertips cut off, which internet trolls love to make fun of when they see pictures of me from back then. I didn't do that to look like some cool tactical badass operator or show off my trigger finger. I did it so I could feel the dog's leash and clasp when I released him. There's just something about that feeling on your fingertips when you're doing tactile stuff with the dog, whether it's messing around with his collar, ████ ████, or releasing him to go tear into someone. Put simply, I needed to feel what I was doing. I also carried bottles of chopped-up food and meat to throw at the stray dogs that would come out of the woodwork during a patrol. Believe it or not, the food would keep them from barking at us.

Then, of course, I had the responsibility for one important asset the SEALs lacked, the sole reason why I operated with them: the dog attached to my waist with a three-foot lead. Military working dogs like Digo gave us a clear and unfair advantage on the battlefield. Without Digo, I wouldn't have been given the opportunity to be operating with these men.

CHAPTER 7
ON COMBAT

My first experience entering a combat zone remains a vivid memory. During my first missions in Iraq, I remember thinking that combat would be similar to all the training that I'd done back in Virginia Beach. While all the training can prepare us for what we'll experience overseas, I don't think it can express the emotions evoked during an actual mission with bullets flying and things exploding. During training, as real as that may seem, we perform one way, but we don't know how we'll actually perform when it's real.

I thought I'd be a little more apprehensive when things started blowing up around me on one of those first missions, but for whatever reason, or maybe because I simply didn't know what to expect, the severity of the situation didn't seem to faze me. I also may not have considered how bad some of the bad guys we went after were. I certainly heard plenty of stories about combat and our objectives. As I received all my gear and kitted up, I felt neither anxiety nor adrenaline. Rather, a sense of excitement overcame my body. I could feel my heart racing.

After a few minutes, that would slow down as we went over to the Joint Operations Command (JOC) to go over the mission. I listened as they laid out everyone's role as well as that of the dogs, and knowing my specific part of the operation helped me feel calm. Because we all considered Digo a maniac, I didn't bring him into the team room, but as soon as we finished, I kitted him up with his vest.

We boarded the helicopters right outside our huts as the whirring blades created enough prop wash to blow away any small thing that wasn't tied down. Based on the mission brief, we expected contact. For the first time in my life, I was about to do something I'd always wanted. I had tried to get close to combat before, but every mission prior to that, we had returned to base with no significant action. I fell asleep on most helicopter rides, but I stayed bright-eyed with excitement on this one. After landing in a field, we formed a circle and waited for the helicopters to take off before the teams moved out on patrol. I made my way to the front so the dog could search ahead of everyone. We never knew what we might walk up to.

From there, we headed toward a little village they called Boy's Town, a nickname for the area because it had no women or children. I asked others why, and they said the bad guys had come in and just taken the shit over. None of the guys had ever seen anything like that before. I didn't know what to expect on that mission, but I can tell you that everything seemed so much slower than in training. We knew that insurgents had rigged many of the houses with IEDs. They were tricky little bastards. Only animals and men in that town. I'm sure some would make jokes about that, but I never would because I saw them doing some not-so-pleasant things to animals. You would think that a religion that prides itself on going to have seventy-two virgins would find someone in real life rather than some animal.

Overall, things didn't seem too bad until we entered the village. Then, it got real. We walked past houses with windows covered up by blankets and sheets. Unusual for sure. It had this eerie feeling, kind of like we were playing hide and seek with kids in the middle of the night out in some scary woods. However, no woods here. The real shit. I didn't realize how real until we reached the target building and started to call the people out. No one exited, so we decided to toss a thermobaric grenade at the doorway that would ultimately blow up the doors and everything around it. Once again, my adrenaline kicked in because everyone in the village would know we had arrived, and the dog would soon be called to go in. A couple of people ended up coming out, but no more, while all kinds of stuff burned in front of the doorway. Then, the team leader called for Digo.

Typically, I would hang out near the gate waiting for them to round up all the people coming out. If I knew that people were coming out, I'd go to the other side. Digo, the opportunist, was always looking for a free bite. Over comms, I would hear my call sign. I would move up to the front of the compound and listen to the radio while those next to me said, "Dog up." The team leader would reply with, "Send it."

On this particular day, Digo went in for what seemed like a long few minutes but was probably much less than that. He came back with no indication of anything, so I sent him a second time. It probably seemed as if I didn't trust my dog because he operated with so little effort in accomplishing a task. However, I figured sending him in for a second search wouldn't hurt.

When Digo came out, the team decided to move up to the building. It's amazing—in a life-threatening situation, everybody seemed to move 75 percent slower than we did in training. It allowed me enough time to get my head on right and proceed to the back of the train and then walk up to the men in the first and second positions. I gave Digo the command to go search again while the rest of the team flowed in.

I stayed in position while three or four assaulters entered. Although up front and willing to go in and clear rooms, my main goal was to keep my eyes open for the dog and figure out how to guide him. The slowness of the operation made that easier. The saying that slow is smooth and smooth is fast seemed true, especially overseas.

As the number one assaulter came out, I poked my head in and redirected the dog as needed. Some might think I was chickenshit for not moving up to the number two, three, or four position in the stack, but I quickly realized that my job was not to clear rooms but to direct the dog to search. In addition, standing in the middle of the hallway was never a smart thing to do. So I would quickly go from room to room after they had been cleared so I could work my way up with Digo. We ended up searching the whole house but found nothing.

The team did discover that they could count on me and Digo. That, in itself, made for an amazing first outing in starting to build credibility with the team. They trusted me and Digo because after we finished searching the whole compound for people, we started clearing the compound for explosives.

Digo and I started sweeping the exterior courtyard working our way back to the building. He was trained to look for components of homemade explosives as well as TNT, dynamite, and other odors. As we worked back to the building, I stopped to send him to an outbuilding that had not been cleared. As he approached it, he began to throw his head up and slowed his pace. When he got to the door threshold, he slammed his nose hard on it, taking a deep sniff before sitting and looking at me. I called EOD over to take a look, and soon after, they were able to get the door open and determine that Digo had indeed found several mortar rounds used for IEDs. That night, the guys learned that Digo would be a valuable asset when it came to finding not only people but explosives.

We linked with the other patrol for our exfil, short for exfiltrate, a fancy way of saying leaving, and rode back to base. As we got on the helicopters to exfil back to base, I felt a huge sigh of relief. Not only had I shaken those first-time jitters, but I'd actually gotten to do what I had gone there to do. I'd also avoided making any mistakes or causing any negative outcomes. Most of the team thought I'd done a great job by staying close enough to use the dog but far enough back to stay out of the way. At any moment, shots from an enemy rifle could have rung out, or an IED could have exploded, and we'd have found ourselves in a firefight. Luckily, it didn't happen that day. However, combat has to begin somewhere, and it certainly would soon.

I wouldn't call that first mission the most exciting. More of a relief. I went on more missions than I can remember throughout Iraq and

Afghanistan during multiple tours. The following chapters will detail many of those. The mix of gunfire, explosions, and death intertwine with so many of them, but some had none of that. However, it was only a matter of time before I'd fire my weapon and kill someone. The movies make it seem so easy as if it's nothing. That's far from reality. It's definitely something. At the end of the day, you're taking a human life, no matter how crappy you might think the other person is. I always felt that whenever we killed somebody, we had fueled the next wave of Taliban or Al-Qaeda. When you think of it, that is somebody's uncle, brother, son, father, you name it. People hated us already, and that one death might multiply that hatred by ten. And so on and so forth.

On the mission when I first killed someone, I peered into a courtyard and saw a guy moving with an AK-47. I'm pretty sure at least one other person shot at him because when I actually got close enough to take a good look at him, his head appeared to be in the shape of a canoe and was smoking. I, for one, was aiming center mass and knew where I'd hit. I know that sounds gruesome, but that is combat, and nothing about it is pretty. All of my rounds landed on the chest because that's what I had aimed for. I had fired about fifteen rounds from an MP7 submachine gun. I'd had to shoot more than simply one normal bullet because of how fast and small the rounds were. The SEALs told me during training that it would not put somebody down as fast as, say, an M4 or HK416. Walking up and looking at someone you just killed makes for a surreal scene to say the least.

For a couple of nights, I thought about how God could forgive me for doing some of the things that I'd done and how I could justify it to myself so I'd no longer feel guilty. At the end of the day, it was either him or me, and I was always going to choose my teammates over the "enemy." I put that in quotations because it's hard to feel that any of those people were our enemies.

Politics aside, we fought the Taliban for years and then simply walked away, leaving them in charge. For example, prior to our entry into Afghanistan, women weren't allowed to do a lot of things. I felt like we tried to change that for the better, and now it's right back to the way it was. I look at my daughter, wife, and other female family or friends and cannot imagine them living under that oppression. Ultimately, those in that country have to want to stand up to their oppressors. Having been on target with some of the local men (not Al-Qaeda or Taliban), I found them very weak. Some of the Afghan Army soldiers seemed scared to even fight. I noticed many brave ones that would step in and do the work, but I certainly never found a majority with the will to fight.

Regarding the man I killed in the courtyard, it was certainly difficult watching all the family members come out crying as soon as they saw their husband or whoever lying on the ground dead. He had every opportunity to come out with his hands up and no gun. Most likely, he would have simply returned to his home after questioning or, at the very most, would have been taken back with us and then released sometime later because that's what happened most often to those who simply complied with our interpreter's callout. Those who didn't, who brandished a weapon, who fired at us or presented an imminent danger went down.

Sometimes, we went after the same person twice. We made it very apparent who we wanted. We gave them ample time to come out and gave them no reason to fight. Surely, they knew soldiers would come and surround their compound. In general, if the guys with beards and little green eyes from NVGs showed up at your house, you knew you may be in some deep shit. You also knew that you had no way out of it. To fight us seemed a bit like suicide.

So the first time I ever fired my weapon in combat, I killed someone. I don't celebrate it. I'm not proud of it. I simply did a job. This happened after I had been blown up. It had nothing to do with vengeance but the realization that I had barely escaped death once and wanted to make damn sure that I wasn't the one resting six feet in the ground.

A chapter titled "On Combat" certainly doesn't seem like the place for humor. But sometimes, we simply had what I call funny, screwed-up stories that only happened in combat zones or otherwise war-torn areas. I certainly didn't intend for the following to happen and did everything to make sure I fixed the situation, but here's one notable anecdote that deserves a place in this book.

I am by no means a doctor or anything close to an expert in anatomy. I don't know the difference between an animal bone and a human bone. Hell, I had never even seen a human bone in real life until…well, you'll see.

We had just finished up a mission. As we patrolled back, we passed through an area that had flags and some other items that didn't register for me at the time. As we walked back to the helicopter, my dog bounded over to me with something in his mouth. At first, I thought he had a thick stick because the ends were kind of chewed up, and I figured he was only doing what dogs do. So I told him to let it go so we could play fetch. It seemed harmless because we were far from any danger and in the middle of nowhere. With that in mind, in the middle of a combat zone, I played fetch with my dog.

Meanwhile, everybody else was kind of laughing. After all, who plays fetch with a dog in Afghanistan on a combat mission? One guy said the stick looked like a bone, but I brushed that comment off, assuming he was kidding. Soon after, we reached the helicopter and returned to base. The dog still had his stupid stick, so I put it up on the wall to make sure he couldn't get to it anymore because I had gotten tired of playing fetch. Even a dog trainer or handler grows weary of playing with the dog.

At some point, one of the medics came by our hooch and saw the stick sitting on the wall. "That's a pretty cool femur bone you have there."

That came as a total shock to me. As it turned out, that other guy had been serious when he'd said it looked like a bone. Even then, I didn't think he'd meant a human bone. I found out that we had been walking near a graveyard but one not marked with headstones as we have in the United States. In Afghanistan, they mark them with things like flags instead. In addition, they sometimes failed to bury their dead deep enough, so wild dogs would claim their newfound "stick."

I thought I might have been in trouble for this, at minimum, or worse— haunted for the rest of my life. In the end, I took the bone to the interpreter to give to the Afghan Army guys to ask if they would properly dispose of it. Of course, I told him not to mention anything about playing fetch with it. The last thing I needed was to get blamed for accidentally messing around with somebody's freaking femur over in Afghanistan.

When those in combat say "that's war," we can apply it to the most tragic or simply to the crazy things that happened. I saw plenty of both.

CHAPTER 8
ENTER DIGO

Digo was a hero. The dog saved lives, and for that, I am forever grateful. So grateful that I tattooed his name on my chest and see him every day in the mirror.

I first met Digo after arriving at SEAL Team ▮ in March 2007. Digo was a misunderstood dog. He needed someone able to communicate with him in a way he'd understand. What worked for other dogs didn't work the same with Digo. He had already taken a few accidental bites. The dog loved biting. It didn't seem that he could help himself. Perhaps unsurprisingly, another squadron had passed Digo to my squadron, and as the new guy, I got paired with him.

At first look, Digo didn't give off the vibe of a maneater. He was sixty-five pounds with a beautiful coat and face. He could have easily modeled for dog food commercials and even appeared in movies because he was that photogenic. He definitely had the look of an underdog.

I had to find Digo's off switch before I did anything else. That was key because Digo wearing a vest and in training created a sight to behold as if Satan had said, "I made a dog and named him Digo." The beast was all animal when it came to working, so I had to tame his aggression.

Basically, we would back-tie the dog to a round wooden table about two and a half feet high, which allowed the dog to be more or less face to face with the decoy. We typically used a pole in the middle so the dog could rotate around the table while we worked with it. The chain connected to the pole extended all the way to the edge of the table so the dog wouldn't fall off. The decoy wore no protective equipment—only clothes that had been bought and worn by people in Afghanistan and Iraq. That taught the dog to go after people on command without the presence of any training equipment.

Foaming at the mouth and snarling barely describes Digo's aggression. In the stack or running with the team, he remained intense and loud. Any gunfire or breach would set him off. I had to work with our trainers constantly to fix that because we had civilian trainers that were prior police officers or K9 handlers. Our handlers would also be sent to different training courses, but we also trained one another. As time went on, they would teach us and then we'd help with the training aspect of starting a dog from the bottom all the way to more advanced work. It's one thing to have a breach go off; it's another to have the enemy know our exact position. I didn't need a dog acting as a barking beacon for the enemy to decide where to point and fire their weapons.

Digo and I deployed to Iraq in January of 2008 in a C-17 military transport plane that would take us from Virginia to Germany and then on to our final destination. I kept him crated because there was no way I'd allow him loose on a plane with a bunch of guys and their gear. Some would allow their dogs out to hang with the guys, but Digo wasn't so lucky.

We landed in Balad and then went to Forward Operating Base (FOB) Warhorse. A plane the size of a C-17 Globemaster couldn't land on the small FOB, so we rode CH-47 Chinook helicopters with all our gear slung underneath. A sight to see for sure. The team gave me and Digo a small room with two twin beds. Instead of a dog bed, Digo simply slept on one of the twin mattresses doing just as he wanted. He loved it.

Most nights, if we didn't go out, we would just sit around the fire and shoot the shit and have a couple beers. I spent most of my time working out and playing video games like *Call of Duty* or *Halo* with the rest of the guys. It was an easy way to pass the time, but unfortunately, due to Digo's nature, he couldn't just be there to hang out. We also had a really tall flagpole that we'd see the terrorists constantly lodge rockets over as if it was a point to aim at on base allowing them to make sure they at least hit the base. That drove Digo crazy. No rest for him meant no rest for me.

Night in and night out, we hunted bad guys—high-value targets (HVTs), terrorists, IED makers, terrorist financiers, or enemies that lurked in the darkness with an AK-47. The macro-mission in Iraq (end Saddam Hussein's reign of terror) and Afghanistan (end Taliban control that harbored Al-Qaeda and ISIS) whittled down to the micro-mission our teams carried. Two countries, same story.

Luis Souffront, our EOD guy, showed me some of the different IEDs we would see. This became a valuable skill, as Digo and I would search for explosives in a compound after others had secured a target, a nerve-racking task because those guys were tricky with the IEDs. I became familiar with the ones that had two saw blades or pieces of metal almost touching. Stepping on them would make a connection and detonate the IED. Another type would use pressure plates under doormats. Walking through the doorway would set off the IED, triggering a world of hurt. The enemy also used what looked like Christmas tree wire rigged to a nearby IED with two wires almost touching. When they connected, they'd blow up the nearby ordnance that it was attached to. I remained forever grateful to have met Luis for the knowledge he shared with me. We were in Baqubah, Iraq, historically known for its Al-Qaeda presence and prolific use of IEDs in general. Digo and I needed all the help we could get as novices with little knowledge of the various types of IEDs and how they worked.

Typically, we found them around the outside of the building or the wall. ██ ██ Those guys placed IEDs along any nook or cranny, around corners in the middle of the courtyard, and just anywhere that they could fit them, but the front door was their favorite place.

That stuff was real, and you only got one life. It wasn't *Call of Duty*. Anyone deciding to pull a Leeroy Jenkins and just run full tilt into the fray with no regard for safety or even a plan might very well not make it back.

I found that first experience nerve-racking, but luckily, I had a SEAL assigned to me. He also had a dog and basically showed me how I needed to prepare for the mission. Not the basics like how to put on my kit but how to actually look at the target and use the dog. Those guys wanted to get their kill (or capture) on. Running with dogs wasn't crazy new, but it was new enough that they had to trust a dog and a non-SEAL.

I consistently referred to myself as a non-SEAL because I never was one, and in case I forgot, others would remind me of my role. I respected them, but a few select guys at the command could not seem to get past the fact that the SEAL teams had asked us dog handlers to come help in that capacity and that I had volunteered for it.

My team leader started off by taking me to the JOC and showed me how to look at the gridded reference graphics (GRGs). The small overhead picture of the target gave me an idea of how to position myself. He would then demonstrate how to find out how the infil would work and identify the different route challenges I might encounter by talking to our snipers or the reconnaissance (RECCE) guys.

They were really the lead when it came to route planning and infil. It's crazy what I watched some of those guys do. They would plan routes by using old goat paths and then find them later, even when covered in snow, such as in Afghanistan. The RECCE guys also positioned themselves on the roof, on a ladder overlooking a wall, or on a wall overlooking the courtyard. They could relay information to me if they thought we should patrol the dog to our front or could simply inform us how long the hump into the target would take. Depending on the length in, I would carry more or less water and needed enough for two. Fortunately, we operated in a relatively flat area, so I didn't need to worry about mountains in that part of Iraq.

After that briefing, the troop chief would assign us to a team for that mission because that troop had a couple of teams. The number of buildings at the target site would dictate whether one team had the primary target or secondary. From there, we would ask them what they needed or tell them how we could help. They loved using the dog, which made me grateful. It was really awesome, and I continue to get chills today just thinking about it. I can't really explain it, but I miss it. That much I know.

On one particular mission, we sought those responsible for manufacturing and setting up IEDs in and around Baqubah, Iraq. I was absolutely nervous going out with Digo that first time and didn't want to screw anything up—the number one priority on my list. Digo and I took up the rear with one of two teams. I kept my eyes wide open, looking at everything, and watched where I placed my foot each step on the way to the target. The training that I had done prior to deployment kept me grounded. I kept telling myself, *I got this*. In the end, we discovered four to five people on target, but none of them came out to fight. Digo and I handled it well except for a couple of hiccups, but more training fixed that.

Digo, like me, was an underdog. As I briefly mentioned earlier, another squadron had considered him a wildcard and kicked him out. Although he was an amazing dog, his barking and biting problem presented more challenges than some were willing to tolerate. I, on the other hand, welcomed the challenge. I liked that he had this wild side to him. In my eyes, it made him an even better dog. At sixty-five pounds, Digo was considered a little undersized compared with a lot of the other dogs. At first glance, many didn't see him as a monster, but when he went on a search, he put the hurt on anyone that got in his way. That's why some of the SEALs called him the landshark.

During one of our first patrols, we arrived at this little town and found it eerily quiet. Chilling. The good horror movie kind of quiet. I often wonder about those places we explored. I think about how they might have looked before we arrived and how they look now. That always fascinates me.

That night, we moved up to the compound wall and decided we would conduct a callout, essentially announcing an opportunity for anyone to come out before we sent in Digo. We started by throwing a thermobaric grenade. It was damn loud, so anyone who wasn't awake before then would be. It reminded me of the recruit division commanders (RDCs) walking around, banging the damn trash cans to wake us up in the morning. The concussive effects from those grenades amazed me. It would knock doors right open. Those grenades were one huge, "Surprise, motherfuckers, we're here!" They were obnoxiously awesome.

After everyone came out of the building, I sent Digo inside the compound where I could watch him search. Digo always had his nose to the ground with his mouth barely open, but I could still see his little fangs hanging out as he investigated. The uninitiated might have even considered it cute, but they wouldn't if they only knew what that mouth of his could do.

I had trained Digo to follow a little red laser, which would allow anybody with a laser on their weapon to direct the dog into different areas that I couldn't see if I stood at the front gate, for example. Some of those courtyards had a little bit of complexity to them, while some had a simple square shape. We typically had people posted up on all the walls as well as the buildings, which allowed us to use Digo in even more complex situations without having to expose the whole assault team. ███████████████ ███ ███ ████████████████He kept searching until he came out. I then called him back. When he returned to my side, I grabbed him by the handle on his vest and told him to heel as we moved up to the building.

The team leader once again called for the dog.

I replied, "Dog up," as I reached the door.

"Send it," he commanded. So we sent Digo.

Dogs are funny. Even though Digo never found anything the first time, he went back in with the same intent. The dog always thought he'd eventually find a win somewhere in there for him. That's the way we trained. Let the dog win. Let the dog have hope. Don't shut the dog down.

On another operation, the RECCE team leader had me patrol up front with the rest of the snipers and let Digo roam out. I briefly turned away from watching Digo do his thing, and when I looked back, I couldn't see him. Starting to panic, I looked over at one of our snipers (who is a good friend I refer to as the angry Korean; if he ever reads this, he will find it amusing).

I looked over at him and said, "Hey, man, have you seen my dog?" Like in the movie, "Dude, where's my car," but "Dude, where's my dog?"

He looked at me. "What?"

"My dog. Have you seen my dog?"

"Are you fucking with me?" he said on that patrol in the middle of the night. "He's down by your fucking leg."

I looked down, and no shit, there he was. I muttered to myself, "Mutha-fucka." After looking back up at the sky in disbelief, I politely gave Digo the command to go back out. I wanted to say, "Yo, get your ass back out there."

I learned the hard way about the challenge of depth perception under NVGs. I felt embarrassed, but it also taught me an important lesson to look around my feet and watch where I walked. I'd probably find Digo, and hopefully, I wouldn't step on any IEDs.

I thought it worth sharing that not every moment on every mission with the SEAL teams functioned like a Hollywood movie. Sometimes, dumb shit happened. You just had to hope it wasn't the kind of thing that got anyone hurt.

Digo and I received the call to go out another night, but this op worked a little differently in that only one dog was needed. Most of the time, that happened when we only had one target or one target compound but didn't have multiple buildings to search. On that op, I loaded up with Digo on one of the UH-60 helicopters. We planned to land in the middle of a field somewhere in Iraq, not too far away from where we'd stage out of at the base.

As always, as soon as we landed, I started to move away from the helicopter to link up with the team that I'd patrol with. I again worked closely with the snipers as we patrolled with them until we reached the target. We stopped just outside, giving ourselves the chance to get all the ladders and everything else ready. More importantly, this allowed me to make sure that if I needed to make any last-minute adjustments with Digo's vest ████████ ████, I could do that.

We started to roll up to the first target building down a little alleyway as we made our way up. When we made our first callout for anyone inside of the building, several men, women, and children came out, and then the interpreter began to direct them where to go. As usual, we warned that if any women or children remained inside and the dog went in, it would probably bite them. After we determined that no women or children were lingering inside, we began to move up to the compound wall. We threw a thermobaric grenade in to soften anyone still inside and opened all the doors so that Digo could gain access. I gave him the search command, and he began to search the whole compound. When he came back out, ██ ███ I relayed over comms that there could have been some rooms that Digo hadn't hit that I couldn't see.

The assaulters began to move in, and I resent Digo in ahead of them. It was kind of cheating for him to lead, but at the same time, I wanted to give Digo an extra chance to find anybody in there. I considered that a risk well worth it because the last thing I wanted was to have an assaulter injured because my dog had missed somebody. Digo began to move methodically with the team as they cleared room by room while I remained in the four- or five-man spot, trying to direct my dog as much as I could without becoming the number one or number two man in the stack. I knew my own capabilities, and I knew that I wasn't a Navy SEAL. As was expected of me, I focused on the dog, not on clearing, though I had received training on that. Fortunately, Digo did his job, and they did not find anybody in there after that.

That led us to a follow-on target right across the street due to some intel, and we moved to start calling out that building. We always made an extra effort to ensure all people had come out. A man and woman exited with their kids, and again, we warned them that we would soon send the dog, and he'd bite anyone in his path. They claimed no one remained, so we sent Digo in. Ten seconds later, we heard someone shouting.

We entered the compound to investigate the source of the screaming. As we cleared the corner, we saw Digo latched onto a man's arm and a woman beating the dog with a broom. Of course, that only amped up Digo more. While serious, in that moment, it also seemed like one of the most comical things I had ever seen.

I tried to call Digo off, but he was the type of dog that, when in that mode, would not back down. You can chalk it up to bad training or whatever, but at the end of the day, dogs are animals, and sometimes, animals do things that are not ideal. That was war.

I knew what I experienced when my adrenaline pumped, so I can only imagine how much his had elevated in that moment. Digo had just searched another building and found nothing and was amped up by the sound of grenades. That was the only reason I could think of to explain why his drive for prey—in other words, his willingness to bite—had shot through the roof.

The guy continued to fight until we finally brought the interpreter up to command him to stop fighting and instruct the woman to drop the broom she had been hitting Digo with, which had only amped him up even more. Finally, I was able to recall Digo, but some damage had already been done to the guy's arm. It was never my intention to see somebody get bitten by the dog, but at the same time, we dealt with some really bad people. The man and woman had made the choice to stay in the house, so that made them responsible for the result.

On another mission in January 2008, we needed to make entry but had to start on the roof and then go down some stairs. That presented a challenge, as I first needed to get Digo up onto the roof. It would be the first time on deployment that I needed to hand Digo up to someone. *What if Digo decides to bite the sniper on the roof?* I suddenly thought. It was dark out, and you just never know what a dog will do. In the spirit of YOLO (you only live once), I decided that Digo was fine and handed him up.

The sniper took Digo and gave him the rolling R, a search and bite command done by rolling the tongue. It instructs the dog to go out and search for the bad guy and anything else of concern in its path. Anyone would be fair game in that moment, so it was really important for us to make sure we directed the dog into the most productive areas and that the assaulters knew that the dog was out searching. If the dog came up to them, they could redirect him with the rolling R or at the very least call the dog's name so they wouldn't get bitten by the landshark.

A huge sigh of relief came over me when Digo followed their command with no issue. So I proceeded up the ladder.

After the mission, the assaulter said that it had crossed his mind that Digo could have bitten him. He'd heard of Digo's reputation for giving love taps.

"Yeah, I thought he was going to bite you as well, but I said screw it—let's roll," I told him.

His response was, "Asshole," or something very near that.

We had to improvise because when you think everything will go smoothly, it doesn't. It can go sideways in a hurry. I remained hellbent on making sure Digo went in first, and those boys agreed with me. If someone got nipped along the way, I considered that collateral damage that I could live with.

I'll now share one of my absolutely favorite stories of Digo putting the work on a guy. Imagine the only thing a person sees is a dog eating their face and throat, and then they're dead. That became the unfortunate ending for one such insurgent. Digo saved people that night. I can say that without batting an eye and without question. A harsh thought, but such is the reality of war.

That night, we planned to head for a target in a palm grove. Three or so shacks rested between a bunch of trees and reeds that we would have to navigate through. Digo and I would ride on one AH-60 of three helicopters headed toward the objective. Seeing the heavy weapons on target, mission planners made the call to soften up the target with five-hundred-pound bombs and then continue to land on the "Y" rather than directly on the objectives. That just meant that we'd land closer to the objective than we initially planned. The advantage of that was we wouldn't have to walk in, but it also had the disadvantage in that, as soon as we landed, the enemy would gather to either start fighting or run away. The element of surprise would be gone.

We would land a couple hundred meters from the objective and take down anything in our way. A cool plan and all, but because of the number of guys going out, I had to ride on another helicopter. That meant when I landed, I would have to make my way over to the team that I would move with for the objective. The Direct Support Course had taught me how to use comms, navigation, movement, etc., but the nature of this work demanded that we think on our feet. The cadre had trained and prepared us in learning to adapt to a situation and overcome it, but they couldn't help us solve it.

The time came for me to load up Digo with his vest and then put my kit on. Due to the chill in the air, I went with a thermal sweater, which I later regretted because of all the running. Digo and I loaded the helicopter and sat near the door. The helicopters rolled out, and there we waited near the landing zone for about sixty seconds. We flew low enough that after the planes dropped their ordnance on target, we put down quickly. I couldn't really hear them due to the calls over the radio and because I was listening to Metallica's "Enter Sandman." (I'd had the comms guys build a wire for me so I could plug it into my headset while also listening to the radio commands.) Meanwhile, we moved in to land a couple hundred meters out and then were warned about multiple squirters—people who would run from the target and hide. Ah, hide and seek. I knew why I loved that as a kid but enjoyed this more. Now I had a dog. I hide. Digo finds.

As the helicopter landed, I knew that I'd have to provide security and wait until it took off to go find my team. I looked up and saw them right where expected. Another team member pointed his IR laser to the ground, and I booked it there like Forrest Gump. Digo and I made it over to our team, and the team leader made the call to move in and find the men and women who had run from the target while clearing any structures in the way.

Palm leaves covered the ground, hiding trenches below—unnatural for that area. We sent Digo out and then recalled him, at which point we tossed more grenades into those trenches. There was shit going off everywhere. An amazing sight. Adrenaline pumping. We continued to send Digo, and then I saw him barking at a small, collapsed shack. Whatever was inside, Digo wanted it. We couldn't get in for whoever or whatever hid there because it had collapsed, so we kept on moving.

As we continued to search, Digo continued to bark from one point to another with his nose up in the air. From there, he would soon narrow to the scent as Digo worked the scent cone—the imaginary cone or funnel from a large scent area to a narrow point. The bird in the sky signaled that a guy lurked about sixty feet from where Digo hunted. He searched so hard that I knew he was onto something. Every hair on the back of my neck stood up. We then hit this wall of manmade reeds where the enemy combatants had cut them and constructed a wall as a perimeter for their little town. I'm not really sure of their original intent, but it definitely provided them concealment.

Then, confusion set in. Digo had clearly found something, but the asset in the sky kept saying that they saw a guy over in another location from where we stood. Many times on missions, we had planes or helicopters that could spot things we couldn't see. Sometimes, they'd see people moving in a certain direction and then lose them. They'd point us in a general direction, but the dog would become extremely important in pinpointing exactly where to find the person. Technology can work well, but sometimes, we simply needed a dog. Digo barked because he couldn't get to it, or him, or them. However, I needed Digo to stop so the bad guy wouldn't aim whatever weapon he had our way.

Digo pinpointed a guy on the other side of those reeds, the same guy that the asset had said was forty feet away. Because of the cover of the palm groves, we continued receiving best guesses from the asset in the sky, but we would have Digo go search, move downwind, and let Digo work that way. Thus, the confusion. The stopping and restarting.

One of our snipers found a way to the other side of the wall of reeds, and we ran one hundred feet in the opposite direction, tripping over everything just to get there. As soon as we got through to the other side of the palm grove, I grabbed hold of Digo's vest and gave him the command to go search. He threw his head up and bolted, knowing exactly where to go—where he had first indicated on a hidden person. Digo hit that insurgent at full speed, grabbing the man by his throat and face. This guy had dug in like a tick with a small manmade hole to try to conceal himself, but nothing was going to stop the landshark.

It wasn't pretty. Over and over again, Digo attacked. We continued to move forward and approach where Digo and the insurgent fought. Despite my best attempts, I couldn't get Digo to come off, not even with the electronic collar at a distance. At the time, I was about twenty feet or so back, and I was not about to move up to the guy while he had hold of his PKM weapon. I felt a little chickenshit about that, but the dog did his job, and we did ours to evaluate the situation. Being on my first deployment, and not being a SEAL, I didn't feel comfortable taking the shot. The guy kept fighting.

I looked over at our sniper. "I can't get Digo off. You are going to have to take the shot!"

Positioned about five feet away from me, he had his rifle ready. Things in combat don't always go as planned. Even though Digo had this bad guy by the neck, he could still possibly take some of us out with this PKM. Since he refused to surrender, the sniper next to me took him out with Digo still latched to him. Digo kept eating away while that guy ceased fighting.

When we reached the insurgent, we found him in a hole with his loaded PKM machine gun. From that position, he could have easily fired through the wall of reeds and taken out several of our men. Our whole team had stood on one side of that wall while Digo pinpointed the bad guy on the other side.

Finally, I was able to pull Digo off, and we continued with the team. Digo kept searching and throwing his head up but could not pinpoint the location of the next guy. However, soon after, the assault force engaged another insurgent in the reeds, that time hunkered down in a rut. They asked if we could send the dog to find him, so we sent Digo, and he began to engage the guy. As soon as Digo grabbed on, the assault force moved up and put a couple more rounds into the insurgent. He was now as dead as the last one, his AK-47 at his side.

I jumped down the slippery ditch to pull Digo off and immediately fell in waist-deep shit water. It smelled wretched and absolutely covered me. Digo had blood and dirt all over his face, and wouldn't you know, as we climbed out of the ditch, the little bastard went after the guy again, throwing me right back in that foul water. I was pissed and soaking wet. Eventually, I'd find the whole thing funny, but not at that moment. Some of the guys thought it was hilarious, as if I'd pissed my pants, so they took a nice little photo.

I was smoked. Mentally. Physically. Just smoked. A firefight that intense can really wear you down.

When we returned to the base, everyone sounded off about how grateful they felt for Digo and his exploits. We had a running joke that Chuck Norris wore Digo pajamas. Digo was the man. I mean, the dog of all dogs. If there was ever a Chuck Norris of dogs, Digo fit that label perfectly. I remain biased, but it didn't make it any less true. So for every Chuck Norris joke, insert Digo's name.

Once we returned, I checked Digo out. When we had crossed to the other side of the reeds, Digo had cut himself on barbed wire. Nate Hardy, one of the SEALs, helped me muzzle Digo, shave his rear leg toward his ass, and clean up the wound. I certainly didn't want the cut to fester and get infected. This was not an easy task, and I was grateful to Nate for the help.

The next morning, we learned that the asset in the sky had noticed people pulling someone out of the rubble from that collapsed shack. The one we gave up searching through. Digo had been right again.

It was easy to get caught up in those missions, all the highs and lows, but in the background, life back home still went on. For me, only six months prior to that deployment, I had decided to marry Erica. I knew the moment I saw her she was special, and my feelings for her only grew over time. She carried herself differently and didn't take anyone's shit, especially if they were a guy. I watched her dish it back to a lot of men, and that's the type of person I knew I wanted to spend my life with. She cared deeply for others and would do anything for anyone. I found it amazing to watch her.

While on deployment, I tried to call her every day around the same time. She had left the navy after finding out we had a baby—whom we'd later name Jacob—on the way five months prior to me leaving. I wanted to call and make sure she was doing okay. It wasn't easy because I knew I'd likely miss Jacob's birth. Some may find it hard to understand or may even consider me selfish for wanting to remain on deployment and do that work. It's not that I didn't value Erica or my son, but I knew I played an important role with Digo.

One night, I didn't call. I was a dummy for making that pattern of communication, but there was a reason I didn't make that call. That night, we lost two amazing operators, Mike Koch and Nate Hardy, and it still eats me up inside. I keep telling myself that I shouldn't feel that way, but I do.

I barely knew Nate from the previous workup—the training that we had done prior to going on deployment. Even then, I didn't know him that well because, remember, all the information fed to me seemed like sucking water through a fire hose. I thought Nate was an awesome guy, and just like the other guys in Iraq, he treated me like I was one of them. His help with Digo's butt shaving is only one small example.

I only really knew Mike from deployment. He had a great attribute in overall kindness and directed that toward me, leaving a lasting impression. Prior to deployment, the guys all ordered these cool, black, Patagonia-like coats due to the expected cold temperatures. I wasn't on that list to receive a coat because, for the most part, if you're an enabler, meaning you are not a SEAL, you don't get the cool gear unless you're friends with the supply guy.

I walked into the ready room one night while they opened all those boxes. Mike looked over at me. "Hey, did you get a coat?"

"No, I wasn't on the list," I replied.

He took the coat off his back and handed it to me. "No worries. Here, take mine."

Don't get me wrong, the navy had issued me cold weather clothing that would work just fine, but him being willing to literally give me the coat off his back was just something else. I told him I didn't need it and that I appreciated the offer, but he insisted, so I took it. I still have it to this day.

One of the most vivid missions I remember happened to be on the night of the Super Bowl. Not many were excited to go out during the game because, although we looked forward to going out on target, this gave us something a little different to look forward to. . While most of America prepared to watch the Patriots and Giants play that night in 2008, I headed out with Bravo Team. Mike and Nate served on Kilo Team. Digo and I worked about five hundred meters away from Kilo. I knew that, if needed, we could make our way over. They had the SEAL handler and his new dog with them, so at least they had a dog to help if necessary. From what I remember and understand from that night, Digo and I would be on the target building that had the strongest possibility of needing the dog. However, you can plan all you want, but in combat, it can always go the other way.

Unfortunately, we would find out that night why dogs are not 100 percent. You can put your trust in them because they've earned it, but you still can't leave it to them to discover everything. That hurts me to say because I absolutely put all of my trust in Digo to get it done, but it is what it is.

We patrolled, making our way through the buildings. Then, I suddenly noticed a guy come to the back window of his house. I lay down with Digo and watched as the man looked around from where he stood. Digo saw him, but I needed the dog to stay quiet. We couldn't afford to let this man know our position. The guy peered around for a minute and decided to go back in.

I veered off with the Bravo Team and waited for us to get set on the target. While that happened, I looked away from the target and scanned all the other buildings where people slept or waited for us to come knocking. Kilo Team remained over on their target building not too far from us.

After both teams were set, a simultaneous callout happened. My team's target was a smaller building with a wall that we had come across. Almost immediately, someone from the inside started spraying AK rounds out the front door. After a brief exchange of gunfire, the guy inside either threw out a grenade or some other small explosion went off inside the little shack, knocking a couple guys off of the wall surrounding the small building. At that point, we backed off and called in the little birds, which started lighting up the building with their firepower over our heads. I could feel brass falling on top of me. It was surreal, and I could just feel the intense pulsing of my heart and the rush of adrenaline. That building was on fire, and since we knew we had it pretty much secured, we saw no reason to go in.

Just to be sure, we moved to the building next door and called out all the women and kids. Then, we had the men come out as well. None of them looked like they wanted any trouble. But something inside of me felt off. We then told the elder of the house that we had a dog about to go in and search. I made Digo bark to show him we were serious. My memory from that point remains a bit foggy on minor details because of the traumatic experience that would soon take place, resulting in the death of two of my teammates.

I sent Digo in from the front of the courtyard, and from there, he searched the building through and through. In typical fashion, I remember Digo coming out with a pillow in his mouth, shaking it. Sometimes, when dogs did this, it was either because of the scent of the "man" on it or simply because the dog wanted to fulfill his bite. Aside from that, we moved in to search the building. We didn't get too far before comms came over the radio with an update on the other target.

I remember hearing that we had multiple eagles down—not a good thing. Then, we received a call for us to book it over to Kilo's target. Kilo Team had been dealing with a barricaded shooter. Multiple shooters, in fact.

By my understanding, Kilo had two buildings to deal with. A bullet struck one assaulter in the calf in the courtyard, and another assaulter in a different building had engaged a barricaded shooter. Had that latter assaulter not kept moving, he would have been hit by the way he described it.

Mike, Nate, and the other SEAL dog handler had decided to deal with this small shack.

In it lay three bad guys who had hunkered down in the corners and waited. They hid behind a great number of miscellaneous items. The Kilo Team dog had gone into the small building, searched for a second, and then come back out. For whatever reason, the dog hadn't found the insurgents. Looking back, I can imagine how difficult that would have been for a new dog. Tragically, I don't think Mike and Nate had even begun to break the doorway before the shooting rang out.

By the time we arrived, the team had finished taking out the barricaded shooters. Mike and Nate lay on the ground. Before seeing them, I had never witnessed the death of one of our own. As others began to shift Nate, I noticed his head move about with no control, so at that moment, I understood what had happened. We had lost them both.

When we returned to base, I went to my room. I didn't know how to take all that in. I didn't know how to react. Then, my team leader came over and said to come out and have a drink. We raised one—well, a few—to Mike and Nate. The Super Bowl was still on, so we sat down and watched the Patriots lose to the Giants. I believe Nate was a Pats fan.

I have this crappy feeling about the Super Bowl now. I quickly realized while people were out celebrating, those two men had laid down their lives. I think about it every day. Every day, we are enjoying something, and out there somewhere, people are laying it down. Soldiers, police officers, and other first responders are sacrificing their lives so we may enjoy ours. It doesn't matter what day of the calendar the Super Bowl falls on. Anytime I watch it, I relive that night.

Those little things like Nate helping me with Digo and Mike's kindness meant so much to me. I didn't know Mike like his Team Guy buddies, but

I remember him as a humble, cool dude. He didn't treat me like an outsider. As a matter of fact, that entire troop treated me like their own. I felt spoiled because that wasn't the case for other handlers in other squadrons. I craved their support and was grateful for them having my and Digo's back because I'd certainly need it on an upcoming mission.

Hindsight is 20/20, and I often think about that night. Reflecting on those bad things is okay, and that doesn't mean that there's anything wrong dealing with those thoughts. For me, I wonder if. If I had been there that night, would Mike and Nate still be with us? Because I had so much trust in Digo, I without a doubt most certainly say yes, but then I guess I'll never know what my dog would have done or not done.

No doubt that those two heroes would still be with us had the dog found at least one insurgent, but that's neither here nor there. I felt bad for the handler on target and certainly don't blame him or the dog. Those dogs did awesome things, but that was war. Sometimes, the bad guys get their opportunity. I ran with those guys a lot on the targets where they were the main assault team. The whole point of those dogs was to reduce the risk of death to one of the guys. But because of that night, I will always say to not completely put all your trust into those dogs, because at the end of the day, they are an asset but one that can make mistakes.

CHAPTER 9
BURIED

Publicly, I've talked about getting blown up a handful of times. At first, I found it difficult to say much. Going to war, you are prepared to die for your brothers who you are serving with, but you are not prepared for the in-between stuff. Things like recovery and healing, both mentally and physically. Even as I sit here typing this, I can feel the bone in my wrist that never fully healed. When I lay there in a hospital bed—crippled—and heard statements from doctors that I'd never be 100 percent or that I'd never deploy again, I had a hard time comprehending that. Now, on the other side of struggling with PTSD and my injuries, I'd say it took me a good ten years to get through it. I know I'll never fully recover from what happened, but I have a better understanding and healthy, nondestructive ways to cope with it. All this after initially trying to find easy ways to deal with it.

In a few short operations, Digo and I had developed a reputation that we could be a huge asset, and the team found Digo highly reliable. No dog is 100 percent, but you are definitely better with the dog than without. Later, at the end of my last deployment in 2011, I found it a tough pill to swallow that when we tried to win the "hearts and minds" of the Afghanis, they left me and the dog behind on some missions to accommodate political crap.

It wasn't about my performance or the dog but rather weight. On many of those missions, they had to have Afghani soldiers and a female Army soldier on the objective. Weight loads, especially in Afghanistan at higher altitudes, limited how many personnel they could take on a helicopter. So I hated it when they cut me from a chalk load, and I had to watch the boys leave because of some stupid-ass rule that you needed a female to search the women and Afghani soldiers on target to waddle around like a bunch of ducks. That never happened in 2008.

Digo and I were killing it. He was turning out to be an absolute badass. He consistently found explosives or material that the bad guys planned to use. He was just a maniac, finding people and destroying them. Have you ever heard a grown man shriek? I never did until the first time I encountered Digo mauling a man. Do you remember that shit-eating grin the Grinch made when he came up with the plan to steal Christmas from the Whos? That's how I felt every time I had a chance to send Digo out to snatch up someone's soul.

That night, we rode in on Strykers—armored fighting vehicles that were larger than a Humvee but that felt like riding in a sardine can. We planned to hit up Baqubah, Iraq, in the heart of the city. That meant a walk-in through the city, but it was a satisfying one since we were targeting the same network that we had been after for quite some time. Everyone always talked about HBIEDs, but no one really assumed they'd ever get hit by one. At least I didn't. We had monitored the house, and from what we observed, those moving about and around the home weren't avoiding areas where others would have hidden pressure plates or crush wire that would subsequently set off the building.

The SEAL team normally wanted two dog teams on a mission, but with the limited room in the Strykers, they could only take one. They chose me and Digo for a reason. While the other team consisted of a good friend, a current SEAL, they wanted me and Digo. No dog or handler is perfect or will always conduct a successful search. However, the team had a tremendous amount of trust in Digo's reliability, so they chose us for this target with multiple floors. Digo's reputation as the king of searching would come in handy there. He was also king when it came to eating the faces of anyone he pinned to the ground. Digo bit wherever he could. He would latch onto any part of the human body. I saw it all with that dog. I remember him latching onto the groin of one person at one point during that deployment. A real ball crusher.

That night, I did everything that I normally did before preparing to go out. I went to the JOC, visited with my team leaders, and got an idea of how we'd take that building using Digo. Because we'd travel into the city, my team leader gave me his MP5 to use because it was smaller than the M4 assault rifle and would work better since I had the dog.

Next, I went to Digo and dressed him out with his vest. The mesh vest worked well for fast roping and other exercises but had no ballistic capabilities and wasn't considered bulletproof. ▮▮▮▮▮▮▮▮▮▮▮▮▮▮▮▮▮▮ Once done, I kitted myself up. Then, I sat by the fire pit with Digo, breathing in the Iraqi air and thinking about Mike and Nate. They paid the ultimate price. At the very minimum, we only wanted to go out there and give it our all. Give it everything we had.

Everyone gathered around for roll call to make sure we had all hands on deck. We then loaded up in the Strykers. Going out the gate that way elicited a whole different feeling. We felt exposed. We'd heard about people being hit with IEDs that had been placed beside the road or dug underneath it, causing unease to buzz through us. I put a muzzle on Digo because we had a high chance of him getting stepped on in that tiny tin can, which meant a high chance of him biting someone. We barely had room to place our feet! Once we were good to go, we set out on a really long drive.

We reached the vehicle drop-off (VDO) location and exited. I stayed near the front but didn't want Digo roaming out. I wanted us both to be accessible in case we came across any suspected IEDs. We'd trained Digo to find people, but he had also been trained to find IEDs and other explosives. I carried an empty water bottle filled with food to throw at the groups of dogs that would come up to us as we moved. The dogs always tried to screw with Digo, but Digo paid them no attention. It was almost as if Digo knew he was a badass and those Iraqi street dogs weren't worth his time.

Once at the target, we surrounded it with snipers on the roofs and men on the walls. My job as the dog handler meant I stayed out of the way but close by. We kept the dog up front because we believed that he would provide an extra set of skills that would be used to smell bad guys or explosives. So I did what I did best. I hugged a wall and looked at all the windows and neighboring buildings that could present a potential threat. Because Baqubah had a notorious reputation for IEDs, the team leader decided to conduct a callout of the building. We gave those inside the target the opportunity to come out—just give up. Don't fight and all is good. Typically, women would come out first with the children, we'd search them, and then put them in a secure location. The men would come out next. Some of them would get squirrely, but for the most part, if they came out with their hands held high, nothing bad would happen.

All the houses pretty much sat on top of each other and were sandwiched closely together because of the way the metropolitan city had been built. This was unlike some of the other targets we went after that were out in the middle of nowhere in the villages. For the most part, this house looked like one of the thousands built out of rebar and concrete. Blankets and sheets covered many of the windows. Rebar from constructions and wires of all types littered the area. Their housing codes definitely weren't as strict as ours in the U.S. as evidenced by the shoddy electrical work. The target house had a compound wall around it as well as a gate, both made out of concrete.

I planned on the best entry point for Digo to do his thing. I avoided the carport by the door because there were three or four people stacked up over there. If only I could have gotten Digo to go around the bodies and in through the door, we wouldn't have had to get that close. Then again, if he had gone in through the door, he certainly would have been killed, and who knows? The rest of the team may have followed and also been blown up. It's easy to look back, playing out other scenarios and critiquing our decisions, but it isn't useful. The truth is we'll never know what would have happened had I gotten him through the front door. I knew the bay window gave Digo the best option to go in, so we placed ourselves against the wall by that window.

This target went a little sideways. I can't recall the exact order they came out, but one or two men had weapons in their hands. The SEALs dropped them in the doorway. Only then did the women and kids follow. We always had an interpreter with us, and he would tell them who we were and to come out without weapons. That saying "play stupid games and win stupid prizes" captures reality, no matter where you live. The two dead Iraqis found that out the hard way.

The previous gunfire had keyed up Digo, and as soon as he saw women and kids coming out, it lit him straight up. Digo didn't care who you were. He would indiscriminately ruin anyone's day—man, woman, child, old, or young. An equal opportunity tormentor and deliverer of wrath. He was going to get you. That's why I loved that dog. A child could have an AK-47, and Digo wouldn't care. Digo would get his.

After all the women came out, one man remained inside. The younger gal told the interpreter that a bad guy refused to emerge, even after she went back in and tore down all the curtains. Game on. I knew I was going to get some work and a bite tonight. So exciting. Until it wasn't.

Digo had this habit of biting people after they were dead, and two bodies lay in the doorway. I told my team leader that we'd need to get closer to send Digo; otherwise, he'd focus on the bodies. He wouldn't physically eat them, but he'd start to really tear at them. If you've never seen a dog bite a bad person for its job, it is something to marvel at. However, in the spirit of giving it a try, I sent Digo, and in typical Digo fashion, he went right for the dead guys.

Had I not told the team leader we needed to get in closer, we wouldn't have been as exposed because I could have sent Digo in from the gate. However, we had to give Digo the best opportunity to enter efficiently. Intent on keeping Digo away from the doorway, I decided to send him through that big window. I knelt down on both knees next to one of the assaulters in the stack. The call came over that we'd throw a frag in the doorway first to soften up whoever awaited Digo. We always wanted to soften up the target for the dog. That frag gave Digo a better chance if the enemy had guns. I heard the call and ducked my head so that none of the blast from the frag grenade would hit me in the face.

"Frag out!"

Boom!

After it went off, I peered over the window ledge. I felt pressure, and for a split second, I told myself, *This is bad.* Then, it *was* bad. Everything went black.

––––––––––

After experiencing the moments of darkness that appeared after the blast, I can tell you heaven is real. I can honestly say I saw a light. I saw a person. She was peaceful. I have no idea where I went in that moment, but I distinctly remember a glowing face appearing through the black. I recognized a girl whom I'd graduated high school with. Not someone I had known well. We weren't friends or anything like that, so I couldn't for the life of me understand why she, of all people, appeared. We'd probably had a grand total of twenty conversations in high school, and I had not seen her, or even thought of her, in years. But there was her face, floating above me, moments after I'd been blown up. She didn't say anything, and honestly, she didn't need to. She brought me so much peace and comfort in that moment, even as I felt baffled over what was happening.

I saw her again—that is, her picture—during my hospital stay in Chicago weeks after the explosion. I maneuvered into my wheelchair and rolled to the common computer to Google her name and see if I could find her. I needed answers. However, I only discovered her obituary. On that day in Iraq, February 7, 2008, when I saw her, I had no idea that she had died in a car accident in March 2006. I had graduated with her in 2002. To this day, even typing these words gives me chills throughout my body. I tear up thinking about it.

I finally reached out to her mom years later, and wrote her a letter. I needed to tell her that I saw her daughter. She replied with a kind note, and while I don't want to disclose what was said, I will say it brought closure for me. I felt like I was meant to live through that explosion to write that letter to her parents. But honestly, I don't know why she appeared to me other than to do that. I think maybe she wanted me to know things would be alright. She was just so peaceful without saying a word. Maybe she was my guardian angel keeping me from death. I felt at peace. Jesus at that moment sent one of his angels to keep me calm and in the fight because I had more fighting to do. For recovery. For Digo. For my nation.

On that fateful day, we had no prior information that the target inside had rigged the buildings, the courtyard, or any part of the target. No one watching that target had seen any indication that we'd have to deal with an IED. We'd been sent to capture or kill an Al-Qaeda in Iraq (AQI) terrorist. I believe as soon as he heard the grenade go off in the doorway, he decided to play suicide bomber and set off the IED. He likely had thirty to forty pounds of explosive weight—enough to bring down the building. Definitely enough to make us take a step back and rethink how we would do things in the future. He blew that house to pieces, the work of one dickhead terrorist who could have just exited with his hands up instead of the other option, which was to clack off a crap-ton of explosives and blow himself up, leaving me buried alive—barely—underneath it.

Digo was suddenly gone from my side. The power of the explosion had snapped the metal buckle that tethered Digo and me together. I had no clue where I was, and for a second, I forgot that I was on target. My mind played many tricks on me. I thought someone had buried me alive, which wasn't that far from the truth. In my mind, I worried that someone had messed up and put me six feet under, thinking I was dead. However, if I was lying in a coffin, I would have room to move a little. So that wasn't it.

Recognizing I could breathe, I started screaming. Muffled sounds reached me, deafened by the rubble. Finally, I came back to the reality that I was still on target. When it clicked where I was, I managed to get myself somewhat under control. Even though I wasn't a SEAL, I knew they wouldn't have forgotten about me. There was still hope.

Soon, I could make out specks of light in the blackness. Stars? As the SEALs lifted pieces of the rubble off my body, more of the night sky became visible. Suddenly, I saw one of the SEALs, Chuck. Man, was I so happy to see him. At first, they didn't move me. I feebly attempted to shift some of the bricks and debris around me, but I wasn't able to make much progress considering I lay there injured and wrapped in wire. In fact, when I tried moving stuff with my left hand, I realized that it couldn't do anything. Lifting my arm up, I saw my wrist just dangling and thought, *Well, that sucks*. I didn't yet realize that my wrist was the least of my problems.

I would later be horrified to discover the carport had crushed EOD tech Luis Souffront. The one-foot-thick slab of concrete killed him instantly. Fortunately, as I would find out, a SEAL who was also caught in the explosion survived, and we ended up with rooms next to each other at Walter Reed National Military Medical Center, formerly Bethesda Naval Hospital.

They came back to uncover me and removed the debris. I saw both of my legs kind of doing some funky bending. I distinctly remember looking at them and saying to myself, *This isn't right—they aren't supposed to look like that*. I was screwed for sure. I remained in shock and began eating fentanyl lollipops like they were Halloween candy. That served as the modern war version for quick pain relief like the old morphine shot that they gave in prior conflicts. That didn't help when two people decided to move me. They got under each shoulder and attempted to lift me. I felt every bone crunch and started screaming again. That sucked. They hastily put me down. And we waited.

Then, I heard Digo flipping out. He was alive!

The blast had not only separated me and Digo from our three-foot lanyard, but it had thrown him fifteen feet. When they brought Digo back to the base, they would discover he had a crushed nasal cavity and a fractured pelvis. However, while still on target, the guys found him with a brick in his mouth, biting the hell out of it but yelping anytime somebody tried to pick him up. Over and over, they tried to lift him, but he kept trying to bite them and latched onto one of the SEAL's ankles. No SEAL or anyone else could control of him.

Finally, they came over and asked me how they should handle it as I lay there incapacitated. At that point, I didn't really know the extent of my injuries, so it wasn't a bother to me. I went to reach into the left pocket of my cargo pants and was rudely reminded of my broken wrist. Wincing in pain, I reached with my right hand instead and pulled out a mesh muzzle so they could put that on, pick Digo up, and take him out of there. I could still hear him barking and yelping, but I remember to this day the one guy who was able to put the muzzle on that little heathen. When a building blows up and falls on you, I don't think that there's anybody in the world that can function as a dog's best friend, and I certainly couldn't at that moment.

At that point, I felt like Gumby and thought I could simply get up and walk away. At the same time, the SEALs still thought they could lift me up and carry me to the Strykers. We were both wrong. Two more SEALs came over, and then I knew the situation was about to suck some more. All four grabbed a limb and carried me out. It ended with yet more screaming before they ultimately laid me in the Stryker on top of Luis. It sounds morbid, but the thought of being there with Luis kept me warm. I looked over at our medic and asked if he was gone. He nodded his head. War is ugly. I can still clearly see that snapshot of Luis laying there with me partially on top of him.

The Strykers drove us to an open area where the casualty evacuation (CASEVAC) helicopter could come get us. They loaded both of us onto the helicopter, where they then worked on Luis. I blacked out a few times on the way to Balad, where medical staff waited for us to come in. After we landed, they wheeled us into the hospital on carts. One doctor came up to me and asked what my problems were. I explained that my wrist was fucked and my legs were not working. Those were my exact words. In response, he asked me whether anyone had straightened them yet. I explained that they looked pretty straight to me, but he said that I would have known if someone had taken that action. With that being said, he asked two other medical personnel to come over. They both lay on top of me, and he proceeded to grab each foot and give each leg a yank. Shortly before those yanks, I had chewed on a couple of fentanyl lollipops. However, none of that took away the pain. They had given me no other meds at that point.

I certainly don't know what it's like for a woman to go through labor, but I've heard the screaming from the room where that happened. Of course, the difference is that someone chooses to go through labor. Anyway, I can admit that I screamed at that level. I screamed so loudly that I nearly lost my breath. Then, I began to whine like a little bitch, wondering why that shit was happening to me. In that moment, I wanted somebody to put me out of my misery and just make the pain stop. I would have done anything to make the agony end, short of selling my soul to the devil.

Next, the doctors told me I needed an MRI/CT and they had to put me under. I wasn't sure whether I was bleeding out inside from my shattered femurs, but at least I was still alive. Shortly after, a pastor came over and asked if he could pray for me. He prayed, and I went to sleep.

I awoke to find myself in much different clothes than I'd been wearing when I went into the MRI machine. I wore a hospital gown and had a tag on my wrist and braces on my legs encased in metal erector sets.

Then, I saw my command master chief peer in. "Anything I can do?" he asked.

"No, but I do appreciate it," I replied.

"Do you want to call your wife, or do you want me to do it?"

"No, I need to do it."

My kennel master back in Virginia, Joe, another MA, had received a paged message at midnight about the incident, expressing that he needed to go to the base. He looked on the whiteboard and saw the indication that both Digo and I had been killed. He later learned that we'd actually been CASEVAC'd and had survived. I hated that he went through that, but what if my wife had gotten that message?

Trying not cry, I dialed my wife's number and told her that I was alright but there had been an accident. Although it hadn't been an accident at all, I had no better word at the time. I told her that a building had been detonated and that I was hurt pretty bad. When I mentioned I would be taken to Bethesda, she said she'd start packing. Such a bad time because the end of her pregnancy neared. She'd give birth to Jacob just two and half weeks later on February 26. I needed her to stay calm. After all, I was still breathing.

We got off the phone, and my long road to recovery began. It would take nine months to be exact. What were two shattered femurs and a broken wrist?

I got this.

CHAPTER 10
FINDING THE WAY BACK

That didn't mean I wouldn't endure a pity party or two. *I guess this is it,* I thought. Might as well just quit, right? I mean, two shattered femurs and a broken wrist. I wasn't a SEAL or even anything crazy extraordinary— or so I thought at the time. But looking back on it now, I failed to realize how special I was. How special I *am.* I don't mean that arrogantly. We are all special—it's just a matter of recognizing it in ourselves and then doing the hard work to bring it to light. I honestly believe we are all valuable and needed. We all belong. No matter what you are going through and how dark life might seem, remember that you are so damn special.

The thought of ending my life never crossed my mind when I was blown up. After Extortion 17, an event I'll describe later in the book, I literally had my MP7 pressed under my chin, wanting the pain to go away. I simply wanted it to be over with. However, lying in that hospital bed, I knew that this wouldn't be the end of my story. If I did something drastic, my family and friends would be the ones to suffer. I might find peace but leave them with a pile of shit because of that action. I had to tell myself that I am special and taking my own life would be shameful considering what they sacrificed for me. We are not randomly born. We're not a damn fish or rabbit but rather created by a Creator for something special. We aren't here by chance. We aren't some random species but those put on Earth for a special purpose. You are special. I believe that now about you and had to learn that about myself in that brief period when I considered quitting life.

They transferred me to Germany on a big-ass plane where I would sit for a day or so. They had to carry about five of us on stretchers, and several other wounded walked on without assistance. I noticed a few weird looks by everybody because I had an afro and what I would call a beard but what others would call patches. I didn't really talk to anybody other than the nurses and medics on board that cared for me. And I only talked with them about one thing: when they could give me my next meds. At that point, I stayed on such a high that whenever the morphine would start to wear off, I instantly felt pain in my legs. The surgeons had yet to fully repair them, and I had what looked like an external erector set on the side of my legs with screws drilled to my lower and upper femurs holding them together. I also had a cast on my broken wrist, rendering it immobile.

My veterinarian technician, Andy Lacy, greeted me while on his way to Iraq to escort Digo back. I was so grateful that he took the time to come see me and that he'd take care of Digo. Seeing a friendly face provided me with some great comfort. Up to that point, I'd only encountered strangers during the medical stops and flights, although I knew many were right there with me in spirit, if not there physically. I still had my erector set on, and they continued to monitor me. From there, they transferred me by plane to Bethesda, Maryland. I wish I remembered more about the plane ride, but they had me drugged up enough that I slept through most of it. I had flown a C-17 aircraft on the way to Iraq, had flown another out of Iraq, and now flew one across the Atlantic toward Bethesda.

The flights weren't easy. I endured excruciating pain anytime they transferred me. It simply fucking hurt. To make matters worse, they had a junior corpsman helping to move me. Did I say it fucking hurt? I remember one of them tried to pick me up using the rod that extended from the outside of the top of my femur to the bottom of the femur. He literally tried that. I was so pissed. I know that he was only trying to do his job, but it was unbelievably painful to say the least. I am extremely grateful for all the men and women that helped along the way. Honestly, if I needed to lift someone in my condition, I'd grip what made the most sense. So I guess the corpsman saw a handle hanging off this dude's leg and just grabbed it, not even thinking. I think that's the human in us. When something tragic happens, we try to make everything else right and sometimes mess up the little details.

Upon returning to the States, I reunited with my wife. Truth be told, I cried during our emotional reunion. I was happy to learn Erica's pregnancy remained right on track, and I did my best to alleviate her stress.

Erica had become pregnant with Jacob back in July or August 2007. We found out shortly after we married at the end of July that year. I almost thought the command might release me because a young, newly married, expectant father isn't the best scenario to work for the SEAL teams for the first time. Nevertheless, they allowed me to stay. Erica was still in the military at the time and worked toward an early separation due to her pregnancy. She certainly wasn't trying to run away from the military. She worked as an air traffic controller and was damn good at her job. One smart and successful sailor. She probably would have advanced a long way had she stayed in, but talking with her now, she wouldn't have had it any other way. She could tell you the exact time and date we found out about Jacob, but I'm the kind of man who hits rocks with hammers, so all I can recall is that we found out sometime during that summer.

That had posed quite a challenge for us, and I hadn't actually planned to go home during my deployment at some point to go see the birth of my son. However, I ultimately protested that to my team leader. I did not want to leave because I felt Digo provided a high level of success probability to completing any mission over there. Call me naive or whatever, but I believed that he was a rock star and a game changer for any mission we had. Don't get me wrong—all those guys were badasses, but at the same time, if a dog can go in there and save the lives of my brothers, then I would rather use the dog one hundred times over.

Erica remained strong though, and she bravely handled the pregnancy without me while I had training trips and then eventually deployed. After the explosion, I wanted to do my best to relieve her of any stress from my wounded condition, but I believe she didn't need me for that, as she knew everything would turn out okay. She remained so strong through it all.

Being wounded had ramifications beyond the actual damage done to my body. During one session with a case worker, they started talking about medical boards. This was basically the nice way of saying, "Thank you for your service, but because of your wounds, you may not be able to come back to the regular navy, much less return to the SEAL teams." An underdog again. That shit lit a fire. I wasn't about to let anyone determine my future other than myself. I had a long nine months ahead of me.

Over the course of a couple of days, the doctors started with a series of X-rays and other tests. They had quite a challenge before them: putting my femurs, which looked like a Tetris puzzle, back together. I found out that the mortality rate for those with a broken femur, much less two shattered ones, wasn't great. So at that point, I was thinking that I was already winning. The doctors hadn't taken my legs, and I hadn't died yet. Regardless, I vowed that I'd live from the moment they dug me out of that rubble to the moment I finished that first surgery.

Hearing what the doctors planned to do sobered me. In addition to putting a plate on my wrist, they planned to shove two rods down my femurs. If you're curious how they fix a broken femur, feel free to check out a video online. They basically take a drill, hollow out the marrow, and then hammer a pin down the femur. Amazing, huh? As horrifying as that sounds, I had a bigger concern. I hadn't gone poo in like a week and had been pissing through a catheter. No fun. I just wanted to use the damn bathroom. It's incredible how we take the basic things in life for granted.

The day of my surgery came, and I was ready. I didn't know whether I would be okay or not, but I gave it to Jesus. He had the plan. I was just there for the ride. Eighteen hours later, I had no external fixators (erector set), and I did have a new metal plate in my wrist. So I was good to go, right? Nope, not quite. I could still feel my bones grinding. Just because they'd drilled down the middle of my femurs and shoved a rod through them didn't mean the bones stopped moving. I couldn't bend my legs at all. Breaking my femurs had caused all of my joints and muscles to lock up in the affected area, which meant that I would have to train that area of my body all over again to work for basic functions. That was terrible. On top of that, I tested positive for some Iraqi bacteria, and everyone who came in to work on me needed a special yellow gown, gloves, and mask. Wonderful.

Then, the devil greeted me. I'm kidding—sort of. It was my physical therapy tech the day after surgery. She gave me her first command: "Get up."

Get up?

I had only finished surgery the day before. I was pretty sure I needed time to heal. But she said, "You need to walk." Okay, guess my recovery was going to happen a little faster than I realized. They presented me with one of the coolest walkers I'd ever laid eyes on. It had an armrest because I couldn't put two hands on the walker. I'd have to go one-handed for a while. Later on, the guys at the command would present me with an even better walker that had tennis balls on the bottom, a little horn, and also a holster. Funny jokes, and I love those guys for that.

At the urging of my physical therapy tech, I grabbed the bed handle hanging above my head and proceeded to lift myself. Screw me, did that suck balls. Then, I remembered the medical board comment that my career might be over. *Keep going, Benny. Forget the doubters. You got this. Jesus has a plan for you.*

I took my time and swung my legs over the bed and felt the grind of bone on bone and bone on metal. Crying, I stood up for the first time in like a week or so. To give you an idea, it took about fifteen minutes just to lift myself up and swing myself over the bed because of the pain in my legs. It then took another few minutes to actually stand up in the walker and get my bearings. All the while, I sweated profusely and overall found it so demotivating to go from operating in the field to essentially becoming a toddler.

During my first try with the walker, I made it about five feet in twenty minutes, and from there on, I made it a goal to go longer and farther each time. I made those distances faster each time as well. I wasn't going to let this be it for me.

For the next exercise, I lay on my bed while someone physically bent my legs. They would take one hand and push on my foot while the other went under my knee and lifted. Everything was locked in place. If I couldn't get my legs to bend, I'd have to go back in for another surgery to correct it. Sigh.

One day, the nurses wheeled me over to another patient, Jeff, one of the guys with me that night when we got blown up. I believe he had been buried, or partially buried, as well and had suffered several injuries about as severe as mine. It was nice to have him in the room next to me so I didn't feel like I was alone in the hospital at night. We enjoyed talking with one another and would joke about not taking a poop. When enduring a shitty card life deals us, it's comforting to know someone is walking that same road.

I felt humiliated once the catheter was removed. I now had to try to use the bathroom on my own, but first, I had to have someone help my naked ass get there. I started crying, telling the corpsman that no one should have to do this. I also cried to my wife, apologizing for her having to wipe my ass because I couldn't stand on my own two feet to do it by myself. As mortifying as that was, I'm so grateful for the people who did help me.

With everything going on with my legs, I hadn't had a haircut in some time. I had quite the afro going while in Bethesda, so I spent a lot of my day with my hair pick, just combing my hair. You'd be surprised at the stupid mundane shit that you find enjoyment in when you're just lying around in a hospital. My wife even bought me a headband so that I could keep my hair back.

At some point, while I was being wheeled around the hospital, someone important walked toward me. He had two little minions, one Marine and one sailor. I didn't know who he was, and at that moment, I remained in a constant state of high irritation from the pain, and I was struggling mentally. I had worked so hard prior to that deployment to get to where I was, and all of a sudden, I had to learn to walk again.

The guy in civilian clothes stopped the cart that I lay in and said, "Who are you?"

I replied, "Who the hell are you?"

He was Admiral Mike Mullen, chairman of the Joint Chiefs of Staff. His whole staff dropped their jaws. After he told me who he was, I apologized and explained I was just exhausted and struggling. He acted cool though and said he'd be by to see me later. He came by right after I'd just received another dose of painkillers. I lay there in my bed, itching my genitalia. I couldn't help it—morphine just made me crazy itchy. He walked in mid-scratch, and with that same hand, I reached out to greet him. Because he had been so cool before, I gave him a "what's up, bro?" as I stuck out my hand. Without hesitating, he shook my hand. I'll give him that—he didn't judge.

In addition to all the medical care I received, Erica and her mom continued to take on the role of first-class nurses. They changed bandages around the holes from my external fixators. They left them exposed to heal up naturally, and with that came drainage. Honestly, it was gross, but like troopers, they kept at it.

To give you an idea of how much I love soda, I recall when I first saw Erica at the hospital, I asked her for a soda from the vending machine down the hall. Well, there was no vending machine, but due to the sheer amount of medicine in my system, I was sure I'd seen something that wasn't there. Also, when I first saw her, I said, "Don't worry, honey. They gave me an ultrasound, and it's safe to say everything still works downstairs." She laughed and honestly couldn't believe the stuff that was coming out of my mouth.

At some point in the hospital, I was pleasantly surprised to be reunited with Digo. The staff, my family, and the vet tech, Andy Lacy, had concocted a plan where they told the SEAL with me that we needed to get X-rays again. That wasn't out of the norm, so we wheeled around until we reached a corridor, and there sat Digo, waiting for us outside. He wore some bandages and looked like ass, but we all looked like ass. I'd lost so much weight in the hospital, but Digo looked no different. Nonetheless, he did leave his imprint on both Andy and Frank, the kennel master at the time. Digo had managed to give them both a couple of bites due to his ornery nature—not to mention the pain he was experiencing.

On the day of the explosion, Andy had received a call in the evening while at home in Virginia Beach. He'd only been told that one of the forward-deployed dogs had been injured. At that news, he immediately called the kennel master, Frank, and headed to work. He had experienced four calls like that in as many months. Once on base, he made some calls but experienced busy lines and could not get ahold of me, Digo's handler. He found it odd that I wouldn't respond about my own dog and then realized I must have been injured as well. So he went home and packed a bag and flew out that afternoon to Germany. These dogs, the ones in SEAL Team ▇ are the most elite military working dogs, so they not only receive top-notch care, but they are also part of the team. All of us care about them and care for them as we would any team member.

Once in Germany, Andy found out that the veterinarians had continued to work on Digo but thought he might need to be euthanized. However, he asked the colonel there to do everything possible to keep Digo alive. While at Landstuhl Regional Medical Center, Andy came by to see me. I found out later that he had noticed my toes were exposed, but I was also all splinted up. He asked the nurse to borrow toenail polish since he knew I could not outrun him in my condition. Sailors will play pranks on one another. He was an Army guy, and I believed he thought it would be his best chance to get one over on me. Lucky for me, by the time he found some nail polish, they had shipped me to Bethesda.

Andy then flew to Balad, Iraq, and people began offering condolences about Digo. That shocked him because, on his last status call, they'd told him Digo was fine. He arrived at the vet hospital and found Digo sitting between two female vet techs, watching TV. He had an IV in his front leg, wore a foley catheter, and had bandages on his head and hind leg. Digo looked up at him and growled. Typical Digo. Andy's first thought was, *Thank God*, but his second thought was, *This will be a long trip*. He found out that another combat assault dog (CAD) had died during a routine medical procedure that night, and that's what had caused the confusion.

Digo had a fractured sinus cavity, bruised lung, crushed kidney, and fractured pelvis as well as damage to some muscles in one of his hind legs. He would need sedation on Ketamine and would keep the foley in until they reached Germany. Andy removed Digo's IV en route, but the dog was doing okay, so he didn't restart the IV. Shocker—Digo didn't like needles.

Andy took Digo all the way from Iraq to his third-floor apartment in Virginia Beach. He had to be back at the vet hospital at 8 a.m., so he took a shower, after which he found Digo on his bed. With some coaxing, he moved him to a better spot. At that point, Andy had been awake for fifty-six hours. After getting some sleep, he got up and checked on Digo only to discover he had flooded the room with urine. Once he'd cleaned up and gotten ready, he loaded Digo up and arrived at the vet hospital about an hour late.

The major in charge gave him a hard time about his tardiness, but he explained about all the urine and having to clean that up. In response, the major asked if it had been free-flowing or straining. Just as Andy told him he wasn't sure, he looked down and saw Digo had his leg hiked up and was urinating on the major's boot. Andy told him that it looked pretty free-flowing to him!

A short time later is when Andy brought Digo to the hospital to surprise me. It was a very somber moment for everyone. Even the nurses had tears in their eyes. Several of the other guys injured at the same time were brought down in their beds and were able to pet Digo as well.

The veterinarians placed Digo on kennel rest for eight weeks due to the pelvic fracture. After he healed, they began getting him back in shape and working him up. He needed a few other treatments and procedures for a breathing issue and a misaligned pelvis. That last surgery could have ended his career, but he recovered well from all the injuries and was able to redeploy and enjoy life. Andy referred to Digo as the junkyard dog, all scarred up like one but a true fighter.

I'm sure Digo had a hard time going through that. I loved getting to pet him for those few moments. You really feel for the dogs because they have no idea what they are really doing over there, and then they get hurt by a bullet or an explosion. I would like to think that if Digo knew the dangers, he'd still choose to do the job, just as we humans made the decision to go over there. Digo was a warrior, and that's what warriors do.

As much as Erica and I enjoyed being together at Bethesda, we had to make decisions about our future. Erica would give birth, and we'd have a baby to think about. So we made a tough choice and ultimately decided that she needed to go to Illinois where her parents lived to have the baby. It hurt, but I simply couldn't help her in my current state. Her parents would provide more support than I ever could from my hospital bed.

Our next challenge involved finding a way to have me moved from Bethesda to Illinois, closer to Erica. I won't say I pulled some strings, but because of SEAL Team ▓ and the amazing medical staff at Bethesda, my nurse case manager went above and beyond to help me. They managed to find me a transport and all that entailed and moved me to the Rehabilitation Institute of Chicago (RIC). The place was the absolute best, and I remain so grateful.

Before I could move, however, I had to do my part. Just a week and half into my recovery, I learned I could not transfer to that civilian hospital unless I stopped all the painkillers. I could go back on them later, but I couldn't be on a medicine called Dilaudid, which was delivered through an IV once I hit a button. The key to coming off of it meant managing the timer I'd hit to release the medicine.

It already seemed unbearable the way I had to heal and learn how to walk. It was so difficult, but I told myself I could do it. I didn't know what fatherhood would be like, but the thought of not being there even one day for my child, regardless of the circumstances, was more unbearable. After all, I remembered the time without my dad and didn't want my son to experience anything like that. Even though a baby coming into the world wouldn't know who I was, I told myself, *I'm doing it—period. I'm just going to make it happen.*

The doctors pulled the Dilaudid, known to be several times stronger than morphine. Ah, Dilaudid. That shit was good. Felt like I floated on clouds. Plus, they pulled the OxyContin and the Oxycodone. Fortunately, they let me stay on the Vicodin. All these medications did their job, but let me tell you, morphine did it right. Just how I'm talking about it should tell you how addicted I could have gotten in a short time. In fact, later in life, I would get hooked on Vicodin when trying to deal with lingering issues from all of this. My night sweats from my injuries were already bad enough; now I had to suffer the sweating from withdrawals. I felt pain, sadness, and, surprisingly, happiness those next couple of weeks.

Nonetheless, it was definitely a very hard time as Erica left with her mom and started for Illinois, and I stayed in the hospital at Bethesda for a couple more days until my time to leave. A C-130 Hercules transport waited to take me to Chicago, where I'd continue my recovery. It felt like my life had only begun. A baby was about to be born, and in some way, so was I.

I landed in Chicago, far from complete. They had pieced me back together, but emotionally and physically, I remained a wreck. I could still barely walk with a walker or use the bathroom. I felt like an infant who wants to do everything but cannot yet crawl, so they cry for their mommy to pick them up for food or whatever.

I spent many nights lying in that hospital bed crying, and during the day, I just wept inside. Every day was a constant struggle because I faced one challenge after another. I am not afraid to admit that I cried because, looking back on it, that seemed natural and normal. I felt like a pussy—excuse my language—and at the time, I thought I should have been tougher. However, what I did—the actions I took—mattered the most. Every time life hit me with another challenge, I said, "Okay, underdog. Great. Bring it. I got this." The moral of the story, what I truly believe and what I tell anyone, is if you are ever faced with some massive challenge, just say "I got this." Even if you have no idea of how you're going to do it. It's all about feeding your mind with the absolute belief that you can.

When the doctors transferred me, they put me up on the brain injury floor. What the hell? I felt like a prisoner because they monitored my every movement. I couldn't simply get on the elevator and roam around. Ultimately, I learned a form of empathy that only a situation like I found myself in could teach. The guy next door to me moaned all night and was just out of it. It was obvious that he was badly hurt, and because of the number of wounds, he was now in a mentally impaired state. As he moaned all night, it brought perspective into my own situation and prompted me to realize that things could be much worse. Things could absolutely be worse, but God had spared me and allowed me another chance to become a better person.

An odd challenge came to me next. Call me bigoted, but in reality, we had been fighting terrorists. Al-Qaeda. Muslim extremists. Whatever you want to call them. On my second day in the brain injury ward, a Muslim family came strolling in wearing full burkas and traditional Muslim dress. They had flown their family member who had a bad brain injury from Kuwait to RIC because they wanted the best facility. Instead of getting angry and frustrated thinking of my teammates killed overseas, I had to reason with my own brain that not all of them are bad. Yeah, I said that. We live in America, and what makes America great is that anyone can pay to receive the best healthcare. Even people from Kuwait.

I had to deal with my own situation. Namely, nightmares and night sweats. For some reason, after my surgery, my body would just run hot all night, no matter the room temperature. My nightmares consisted of getting blown up and not being able to walk, all the way to multiple women in burkas with eyes lit red like fire. Still, I wasn't going to let my nightmares control my rehabilitation. My brain was going through a lot at the time, and I just had to tell myself that wasn't reality. I continually pushed forward each day because I had a wife and son to live for, but I also found it hard being away from Virginia Beach. The rest of the guys lived and worked there, and I wanted to live and work there with them, but I had my family to think about, and being with them was best for all of us.

Every day began with me waking up and immediately trying to do some walking exercises. The nurses would bring me food, but I really wanted to walk to the place where we ate because I felt like I needed to earn it. After that, we would do some type of cognitive exercise to work out my brain. We would then go to the physical therapist, who would put me to the test. She would lay me flat on my back and attempt to bend my knees so that my foot would move closer to my ass. To start off, my knee was locked straight—it wouldn't move a bit. Everything was tight. Finally, she had it looking more like an obtuse angle. Great progress, but still not enough. On the plus side, walking became easier, and my legs were getting stronger again. I no longer had days of taking five minutes to move twenty feet. I soon asked to put tennis balls on the feet of my walker so I could scoot faster. The request was denied, but they at least knew my determination.

A couple of weeks after getting to RIC, my wife went into labor. My father-in-law and Zach, my wife's cousin, came to get me from RIC to take me to the hospital. It was forty minutes south, a long ride, but hospital administration granted my request to go and see the birth of my son, Jacob. When they loaded me up, they had to scoot the front seat as far back as they could. I couldn't bend my legs enough to fit as one normally would. Even with the seat moved all the way back, I still had to lean the top part of the seat back so I could fit.

Apparently, there are some doctors who refuse to take pregnant women if they have not been working with them throughout their whole pregnancy. Fortunately, I was lucky enough to find a doctor who understood our unique situation and agreed to take my wife as a client at eight and a half months pregnant. I'm extremely grateful that he did because we sure needed it.

A few hours after I arrived at the hospital, Erica gave birth to Jacob. He was such a perfect baby. The kid never cried about anything and is, to this day, such a lover. He wants nothing more than to do the right thing. I couldn't believe that God had spared me and allowed me to see that. Without God, I wouldn't be writing this book. I owe it all to him.

A few days later, my teammates surprised me. The medical officer at the command wanted to check on my progress, so he sent along some of the boys. Remember, I was an MA, not a SEAL, and here they came out to see me. At that point, I just really felt like they thought of me as one of their own. Of course, a couple of MAs came to visit me as well, including a man who kind of mentored me through the different schools when I first came to the command. From the moment I arrived, that chief petty officer and MA took it upon himself to help me and guide me through the different courses. It was a heartwarming moment when they all came. I don't want to sound melodramatic, but I felt isolated in that hospital with no one who understood how I felt and what I had been through. But these guys…they understood.

When they left, I returned to my quest for Benito 2.0. At some point, I realized that I would never equal my old self. I had to accept that in order to move on. One good thing about healing so far away from the navy in a civilian hospital was that I didn't have to hear about medical evaluation boards or being sent back to the regular navy to finish out my time. That allowed me to push as hard as wanted, and I did. Eventually, I was going to be discharged from RIC and placed in outpatient care so I could continue my rehab.

I had this outpatient therapist named Arpna in Chicago. She was a badass when it came to her job. She pushed me hard, and I embraced that because I wanted to get back to my old self. Sometimes, however, I would irritate her because right when she would turn her head, I would turn up the treadmill or do something stupid because I thought I needed to push even harder. She was a ball buster, but man, what a great therapist. I didn't need someone to treat me like all the other patients. I needed someone to push me hard.

Summer came, and I was ready to go back to Virginia Beach with my family. For me, it only seemed right that I returned to the command and got back up on that horse. When I first returned, I was asked to speak to the support course class that I had gone through. Being a direct support guy, I think the SEAL cadre thought hearing my story would provide a heavy dose of reality to those taking the class. These guys had other jobs in the navy and would work with the SEALs on target or in some other capacity, so it would definitely resonate with them. I went in there and explained how I valued everything taught in the course. Plus, I shared that what I'd learned had helped me survive so that I could stand before them that day. It all made a difference.

A short time later, Lou Langlais, my support course cadre, pulled me aside and asked what my plans were.

"I'm coming back."

He just smiled at me and said, "Really?"

Lou encouraged me to keep pushing and keep the faith. He believed that I could achieve my goal as long as I was willing to do what it took to make that happen.

I started carrying around a seventy-pound rucksack that was basically a sandbag in a backpack, even though all my gear combined was only about forty to fifty pounds. I knew that my legs presented my biggest weakness, and if I planned to make it, my legs had to become my biggest asset. I rucked seventy pounds every day, three to ten miles. *I still have it*, I'd think to myself. I knew I would never likely have a situation where I had to ruck ten miles, but I knew that if I went back overseas, I needed to keep up with those SEALs on the patrols or just chasing squirters. It took me eight months from the time I got hurt to be able to get to where I needed to be.

Finally, in November of 2008, I said, "I'm ready."

Put me in, Coach.

––––––––––––

But first, it's important to share what else fueled my fire. Within the pages of this chapter, a great number of experiences unfold. It traces the intricate path of my life, beginning with the fateful moment I found myself critically wounded in that unforgiving war in Iraq. The narrative then takes you across continents, as I lived through the harsh realities of the battlefield before shifting to the gentler surroundings of a hospital in Germany. From there, I went to Bethesda Naval Hospital in Maryland and eventually to rehab at the Rehabilitation Institute of Chicago. This chapter is the culmination of all those moments.

However, amid the chaos of war and the struggles of recovery, one figure emerges, a person of unwavering support and love—my wife, Erica. Her story, also an incredible journey from a youthful twenty-year-old to a steadfast partner and expectant mother, unfolds with mine. The burdens she bore wore on her as heavy as my injuries, the anxiety of my absence, the strain of my deployment, and the sheer gravity of the situation. And when fate dealt its harshest blow, when I lay there, left shattered by an explosion, Erica rose above her own fears and uncertainties, using her strength to hold back her emotions and tend to me with care and determination.

The anecdotes we hear about wounded warriors are often tales of isolation, where days melt into one another before a familiar face graces their bedside. Erica shattered that mold. Defying the odds, she stood by my side with resolute devotion. She could have easily turned away, choosing an easier life. A path less rocky. Yet she chose differently. She clung to the promise of 'til death do us part and the dream of a family succeeding against all odds. With her courageous heart, she faced the monumental task of caring for me, all while pregnant.

I am driven to speak this truth: my continued existence, my presence in this very moment, is the result of God's unwavering love. It is as though the universe conspired to align our paths and place Erica in my life when I needed her most. The orchestration of these events goes beyond coincidence, as God's divine hand guided us through dangerous waters. My gratitude extends not only to the Lord but to Erica, the embodiment of grace and strength, who stood by me when my world seemed to crumble.

CHAPTER 11
BRESTON: REDEMPTION

In September or October of 2008, Digo went overseas with his new handler. That made part of me sad, but another part of me was happy for Digo. I was disheartened because all along during my recovery and his recovery, I thought we might redeploy together. I didn't think we had finished our story. Digo operated like a heat-seeking missile and could find just about anything he went after. If someone hid, he'd find them. If someone hid something, he'd find that thing. Those dogs are so smart, and when paired with the right handler, they are unstoppable. Despite my hopes, I knew that they had made the best move for the squadron, and I also knew that it gave Digo an opportunity to get back out there. It was best for me, and I had to accept that. Although it made me sad, it would have been unfair for me to hold him back, not that the military was going to give me a choice.

Accepting that Digo had deployed without me renewed my motivation to get back to full health. I continued to push myself even harder for the next two months, not knowing what would come next. Soon enough, an opportunity arose, and I weaseled my way back to deployment. Despite listening to all the comments about what I couldn't do and shouldn't do because of my injuries, naturally, I did the exact opposite. In the words of a very good SEAL friend, "I wouldn't expect one of our own to do what you did, but I certainly wouldn't expect an MA dog handler to do it." That meant a lot to me. People continued to look at Digo and me as underdogs during that whole journey, and we kept on doing what underdogs do—surprising people.

December came, and I heard that Digo was having some issues with the way he went in and searched compounds. He would go in very shallow on buildings to the point where he would not search the whole thing. On multiple occasions, they sent him into doorways, and he went in two feet, turned around, and came right back out. I personally don't feel that was a result of the explosion or anything like that. Dogs will sometimes do things we don't like, and we don't know what causes it. As a dog trainer and handler, I had to recognize that I was dealing with an animal, and they were just going to have a mind of their own sometimes.

During a training trip I went on, we had a SEAL who was a new dog handler. I had the utmost respect for that guy, and he is one of my best friends—or older brother, I'd like to think—to this date. At the time, he served as my team leader for the dogs in the squadron. The big, angry Korean, as I called that guy, had a dog that kept messing up.

He came to me and asked, "Why does the dog keep doing that?"

"It's a dog. They do that sometimes," I said, simply because I had no other answer. In situations like that, you often had to chalk it up to the fact it was just an animal.

Unhappy with that response, he proceeded to chew me out in front of all the new ██████ Team guys. At the time, it scared the hell out of me. I'd never seen him get quite as pissed as he did, and to get that hammering in front of the new SEALs at the command humbled me, but I took it. Comically though, I think they were thinking "oh, shit" and began to make themselves scarce while he finished. Later, I think he understood what I meant by it's an animal and sometimes you can't control it like you can with a computer. You can't diagnose the problem as simply as you'd perhaps like. Thinking about my statement, I didn't like the sound of it, and I wanted to help. I wanted to show we could turn dogs like that around.

My leadership wanted to swap Digo out for a dog named Breston, and that is where I saw my opportunity. Breston wasn't my dog but was later paired with me by my own doing. Breston was a stocky Malinois and had the same coloring as Digo. I was a seasoned handler, and they needed a dog to do the work. I also saw the opportunity to go assist them and see if we could fix Digo while I was over there. After all, I knew that dog well, and I was confident I could figure it out.

With that in mind, I went to my leadership and pleaded with them to let me deploy with Breston. Unfortunately, they didn't want to hear it. They simply wanted me to swap out Digo for Breston. Although Digo was working with a new handler, I explained that I could easily take any dog and make them work as long as they had a little seasoning to them (a deployment or two). Any handler could do that provided they had learned to read enough dogs.

Apparently, that got through to them because my leadership came back and asked if the doctors had medically cleared me. I knew I was good and said yes. Technically speaking, I wasn't cleared, and I wasn't about to redeploy if I didn't get signed off officially, but I just decided I'd figure all of that out later. First step—get the green light. So, yeah, I lied. I lied right through my damn teeth. I hadn't gotten anything signed yet, stating I was ready to go, but I would get that taken care of shortly.

I was about 90 percent healthy. I didn't know what 100 percent looked or felt like, but I sure as hell wasn't going to wait another year to find out. Immediately after I begged them to let me go, and they agreed, I went to the physical therapist and my surgeon, and they signed me off as fit for full duty. No one had pulled any strings. I was as ready as I could be, and they knew it.

Only I knew my body. Someone might question whether I could have put the team at risk or something like that in my quest to deploy again, but the simple answer is no. I knew plenty of guys that deployed after getting hurt and were never 100 percent. Sometimes, the body won't ever reach 100 percent and I didn't think mine ever would. It's something we had to account for personally and push through. What matters is the mind and heart of the individual. For me, I knew I had the heart to go out there and get it done. I knew that mental determination would take my body to wherever it needed to be physically.

I had only a week to get ready with Breston before we were scheduled to hop on the next rotator out. Over that week, I had a chance to really work with him and get him to the point where I knew him and his signs. I could always tell his next move. A great handler must be able to read their dog before the dog takes action. Those dogs loved to work, and they'd work themselves dead if we let them. Digo had no chill mode, and Breston followed suit. Both of his previous handlers had done an amazing job of telling me all the things I needed to know about him. Breston was a badass, and he was one of only a few dogs I knew that had survived getting hit with an AK-47 round. Nonetheless, Breston continued the fight.

The day came for Breston and I to leave, and we traveled to Kandahar, Afghanistan. Jacob was ten months old, and I don't believe Erica agreed with me going, but I did it anyway. It was selfish, but she accepted that I needed to get back there. I would not be the man I am today if I didn't get back to it. I would soon reunite with the SEAL team that I'd worked so hard with in Iraq. When I arrived, they had left on an operation. I had literally just missed them, but it allowed me time to settle in. I walked outside, looked up at the dark night sky, and realized I had made it. Back in it. I just took time to breathe the shit air in. No matter how terrible it smelled, it was great to be back. All the doctors, admin staff, and others who'd said it wasn't possible were wrong. I know they'd only tried to help and give an honest assessment of what my future looked like, but they just didn't know me. They viewed me as an underdog.

Once the team returned from the operation, many shocked faces looked back at me, but they were certainly happy. Watching them on target on a TV screen and then seeing them walk in was one of the happiest times of my life. It was amazing to see all those familiar faces. It reminded me of *The Lord of the Rings* when Frodo wakes up in Rivendell, the elven home, and sees all his homies again after he defeats Sauron. Kidding! Just a little humor for all you fantasy nerds out there. But you get what I mean.

I did get to see Digo during that time, but he looked like a different dog. Like me, he was all jacked up. He had one floppy ear and a scar on his face—he was one mean-looking, ugly bastard. I still loved him though. My wife would say that about me as well.

One of the SEALs walked up to me and said, "We heard you were coming to bring out another dog."

"No! I'm no courier. I came to work that dog," I responded, pointing to Breston. "I'm good to go."

This was the same SEAL who told me he never expected me to crawl my way back to the squadron. He could see a SEAL Team Guy do it, but not me. I wanted it bad though. I wanted to prove to myself and everyone else that nothing was impossible.

I kitted up for the first time since the explosion, and it felt extremely good to return to those missions. I had a sense of nervousness though because this was for real, and my legs would have a huge test in the coming day. That night, however, we flew out on CH-47s and landed about three kilometers from the target with a short walk-in. Never in my life did I have as much pleasure as I experienced walking into the back of one of those helicopters that day. Breathing in the exhaust from the jet-fueled engines lit a fire in me. I enjoyed a sense of familiarity. Of accomplishment in returning.

On that particular mission, we planned to go after some low-level Taliban fighters in the area. They had been tracked to a compound, and we planned for another capture or kill mission. People would like to think that anytime we went out, we went after the big guys, but the fact of the matter was that did not happen every time. Often, we would rotate with the United States Army Rangers on our FOB and take turns going out.

The helicopters took us to our infil point, and Breston and I patrolled up front with RECCE. I had returned with a new dog. I wanted to destroy something—or someone rather—and I had the dog to do it: Breston, an absolute monster. The walk-in was a piece of cake. I had worked my legs incredibly hard during recovery to prepare for this. Rucking those seventy pounds every day as part of my training six months prior to that paid off.

However, I knew that was more weight than I would ever carry with my kit and gun combined, but I was like, screw it, I'm going to carry the kitchen sink if I have to in order to get back to work. I forgot that my mind would present its own challenge, and it had other ideas. When I got on target, it took me a second to tell myself that those buildings weren't going to blow up and that I would be okay. At least, that was what I wanted to believe. The fact is there's always going to be doubt, but when you have Jesus on your side, nothing else matters. Sure, Jesus didn't stop a building from blowing up, but I reminded myself that "he's got me." I could do this.

And just like that, the assaulters started clearing rooms, and there I worked, chucking Breston into several doorways to search. It went like clockwork. Breston would go into a room, search, and come back out, and I would then send him into another room. It turned out to be a really great first operation for my return, and I couldn't have been happier. Breston didn't miss a thing. He didn't actually find anything, but that's because there was nothing to find. It instilled a level of confidence in me that only the battlefield could provide.

A couple of nights later, another operation put my legs to the test. Like *really* to the test. The plan called for us to land in a bowl—mountainous terrain with surrounding hills. We would have to walk our way out of there on these little goat paths that our RECCE guys had found on a map, essentially a herder's trail to the target. When I did my normal walks in and out of the JOC, they told me that it wasn't too bad and that a light three inches of snow had fallen on the ground. The thought of snow actually seemed nice. Snow-covered mountains brought a peaceful scene, or the perception of one, as we walked through dangerous areas. With all that in mind, I put on gaiters to keep my feet dry and warm as well as some other warm clothing because I could always strip down if I got too hot.

Just like any other night, I hopped in the helicopter, put on some music, and fell asleep for a short period until I heard the calls coming out over the radio telling us how far out we were. The call came in that we had thirty seconds to land, so I got ready with Breston. As the helicopter landed, I noticed the boys weren't going out as fast. Or at least when they were going out, it looked as though they were moving in slow motion. Something seemed different.

Next came my turn. I pulled down my NODs, and they messed with my depth perception. I jumped out of the helicopter and expected three inches of snow that turned out to be more like three feet. Nearly up to my waist. Pretty amazing. Then, my brain actually clicked into what was coming next. We had to walk through waist-deep snow most of the way in. We were essentially in the middle of the bowl and now needed to hike to the rim.

The walk-in sucked ass. The expected nice walk through the mountains became an ultimate suck fest. Traveling with Breston made it even harder, so I unclipped him from his leash and let him go. He had a blast. It soon got to a point where he could walk on top of the hard pack and no longer got buried in the snow. I felt bad for the people carrying the ladders and comms equipment because climbing out of that place was miserable. Like Charles Barkley would say, "It was *turrible.*" As much as it sucked, I found myself laughing at one of my good friends, our sniper, the angry Korean. Fun fact about him is that I would find out a couple days later that he was actually Korean. I assumed he was Mexican and when I asked him "what are you Mexican" he looked over at me and said no asshole I'm Korean. He cussed up a storm the whole way up. Absolutely hilarious. Hearing him the whole time made the walk just that little bit more enjoyable. Laughing about a crappy situation often makes hard times better for me.

After we emerged from the bowl, the snow became less deep, and before long, I could see the village. I began to reorient my brain to how I'd viewed the village laid out on the map and on the monitors in the JOC. We soon reached the target and began to conduct callouts on several buildings. The call then came to send the dog into the first complex. I sent Breston in, but he found no one because everyone had vacated when called out. He searched systematically, and I found it really cool to watch him from a distance.

We then learned that two men stayed in another building about one hundred meters away. We were told that they were armed and were not from that area. That almost certainly meant they were not great people.

Squirters started running from another building and into the mountain areas with rocket-propelled grenades (RPGs) and other heavy weapons. Game on! I thought for sure we'd get some squirter action, but it turned out they would be dealt with in orderly fashion versus sucking half our troop up into terrain that they knew. Sometime shortly after, aircraft dropped four five-hundred-pound bombs onto them to take care of that issue. I found it pretty jaw-dropping to see those things take out people from a distance. You could look out and just see big explosions up on the mountainside where they'd dropped those things. I didn't feel the blast wave due to the distance, but at the same time, I definitely sensed some big booms.

We then made our way over to that building with the two bad guys. We sent Breston in ████████████████, and he made his way through the building, searching room after room until he reached a little closed-off area. There, we saw Breston grab a guy by his ankle. Although the guy was kicking him, Breston stayed on.

For what seemed like a couple of minutes but, in reality, was only seconds, we saw a second guy fighting with Breston as well. Since he was outnumbered, we called off Breston, and to my surprise, he obeyed. In my head, I was like, *No shit, he actually came off.* Up until that point, I had only witnessed Digo doing his own little hellion shit where if he had a real solid bite, it seemed like he would just give me the middle finger if I commanded him to let go.

We could see through the window ████████████████ that there were multiple weapons in the room. We conducted a callout for the targets to come out or we would send the dog back in. When they responded by playing possum, we opted to send Breston in for another bite. That followed our normal procedure as we tried to use the least amount of force possible to get what we needed done.

Breston entered again and started biting at one guy's torso. Then came the moment when a different fighter grabbed up the nearest assault rifle.

Immediately, one of our assaulters fired two precise shots that put an end to that threat. With Breston still going to town on the body, the interpreter told the last guy to come out and not grab anything. What do you think he did? He grabbed the damn gun. To this day, I do not understand why. The same result occurred as our guy put him down as well.

After two assaulters cleared the room, I entered. Breston had done a great job staying engaged. He kept at one of the bodies, so I decided to go in and choke him off the bite. That made the dog more engaged with the act, and I knew it would make him even more committed the next time. The last thing I wanted was for the dog to assume at some point I was going to call him off and develop a problem with letting go. When it was safe, I would often leave a dog on a bite longer. I'd go up and grab his collar and slap him on the ass, telling him "good boy" while he got a deeper and fuller bite. At some point, I would grab up the collar with both hands and slowly choke him off, making him want it more and more.

Once he'd let go, I pulled Breston to a cleared room and started to look him over for injuries. I found nothing. We did an amazing job that night. Breston made me so proud, and honestly, I felt pride in myself for doing the walk while Breston did the work. That night put my body to the test, and it passed. I couldn't have felt any more pleased with my recovery.

A couple nights later, we went out again, but that time, we had much less snow to contend with. It still covered the ground but had become hard packed. We had a three-and-a-half-kilometer walk, which wasn't very long. It gave me enough time to look at the terrain and just take it all in. I've said it a thousand times, and I'll say it again—Afghanistan is a beautiful country. It's a damn shame that the people can't truly enjoy it. They have been fighting for so long, and the Taliban makes it impossible for them to relish the beauty of that land.

We reached the target undetected and initiated a callout on one of the buildings. People exited with no issue, and we started to clear it with Breston. He ran in and began searching. Everything went smoothly. The next building, not so much. We called everyone out, and again, people came out with no problem. We moved up to the building, and I knelt down with Breston next to another assaulter. The dog was amped up from the callout and the search of the previous building, so what happened next was an understandable accident.

As I knelt down next to the assaulter, Breston looked over at the guy's calf and gave it a quick little nip. He made a good bite but didn't break skin. The guy gave out a little, "Ah, damn it." The excitement had simply overcome Breston. I'm glad the bite wasn't more serious, and I still laugh at it to this day. The assaulter he bit was one of the most understanding guys I've ever met, so naturally, he wasn't too mad.

After that quick "got ya, bitch" (Dave Chapelle voice) incident, we sent Breston into the building. I followed his path ████████████████████ ████████████. When he got to the last room, he found a man and started to engage. Then, I could see other faces in the background and the sound of screaming. The man attempted to shield his family which, while noble, put him in the firing line of Breston's teeth, and Breston wasn't a dog to be taken lightly.

We called off Breston from a distance and, once again, asked the people to come out. We also reiterated that if they didn't, the dog would go back in and come straight at them. Thankfully, they got the message and complied. Breston made me proud that night. He did everything I asked like a pro— well, except for that little nip.

How crazy that local guy would have been to refuse to cooperate when a bunch of badass killers were at the door, saying they were about to send in a dog who knew the term "sic balls." Crazy enough to go full Allahu Akbar on us, I was pretty sure of that. Okay, I lied. I didn't teach my dogs "sic balls." But my buddy, John Douangdara, whom we called Jet Li and who would die in 2011's Extortion 17 helicopter crash, sometimes told his dog to "sic balls" when he sent him in on a bite, which always cracked up the SEALs he operated with. There are people who sit back at the JOC or in Washington, D.C., and scrutinize everything we do, such as teaching a dog to "sic balls." But those commanders and politicians back home aren't in theater. They aren't facing potentially barricaded terrorists in suicide vests. Easy for them to armchair quarterback.

Another night, we went riding in with the Rangers. The Rangers have a storied past predating the Revolutionary War, and they famously climbed the cliffs of Pointe du Hoc at Omaha Beach on D-Day. I went on several missions with them because in 2009, they had not built up their dog corps yet to the point that they consistently had a dog available. I actually loved going out with the Rangers because they assumed I served as a SEAL rather than an MA. So when it came down to using the dogs, none of them really said anything to me as far as what not to do. I could almost always push my way up to the front and release the dog when the situation dictated it, and none of them would think twice about it. I found that really cool of them. They were a lot of really young guys who just kicked ass.

I remember watching those guys carry damn near everything but the kitchen sink to the target. I'd see a guy with a saw and a ladder. I thought that was crazy because I carried my little MP7 peashooter in later deployments and these guys had all their gear plus all that extra stuff. I didn't even have side plates to protect my vital areas. I know—a stupid decision, but I needed a lighter load when chasing people up in mountains. Sometimes, it is what it is.

This particular mission became the first time in my career that I worked with the Rangers, but they used similar tactics to the SEALs, so I found it a pretty easy transition. When we got off the helicopter, I found the RECCE element and let Breston off leash to roam. We had a pretty easy walk-in. The Rangers just let us do our thing since they didn't have a lot of experience working with a dog. I sensed a little uneasiness from one of the guys up front. I wasn't surprised. They'd heard stories of dogs ripping people to shreds. True stories, by the way. Those dogs could fillet the skin off a person the way some people fillet a fish.

Breston stayed under control and just kept bouncing back and forth from about fifty to seventy-five meters in front of the troop all the way to the objective ready point (ORP). I then reeled Breston in and adjusted his vest. We reached the compound entrance, and just like with the SEALs, the Rangers conducted a callout of all the people in the compound. One by one, they slowly came out. We then sent Breston in, and he started to clear the rooms one at a time until he got to a room where we could hear a guy screaming.

I found deploying the dog to be a tough call because I had never worked with those Rangers before, and they began to systematically work their way to the screaming guy. As they worked, I followed behind about five guys deep until only another guy and I stood alone. Normally, I would never find myself in a situation having to clear the room while my dog was latched onto someone, but again, these Rangers had a different method.

The other guy panned to the right of the room on my side, and I panned to the left of his side on the doorway. He gave me a quick nod and then broke the doorway entry while I made mine. We cleared the room while Breston pinned the guy on the floor. I told the Ranger that I had to move in to pull Breston off but then decided to call him off instead. Shortly after, other Rangers moved into the room and secured the guy while I took Breston out and finished helping clear the compound.

While all that happened, we had another matter. The Rangers worked out of a different base than me, so when I came out with them, I loaded on their helicopter. My team boarded theirs, and we would hit two targets near each other. The helicopters that brought us in did double duty to exfil them out of the same area with some gap in between. As I left the target with the Rangers, I knew at some point I had to walk about 150 meters or so on my own and join my guys.

Naturally, my comms had gone out when I needed them the most. Once I saw my team off in the distance, I broke away from the Rangers to link back up with my guys. Well, what I thought was 150 meters turned into me walking almost three hundred meters on my own. Not the brightest move. ████████████████████████████████████ ████████████████████████ When I finally got to them, one of the guys asked where I'd come from. I replied that I'd walked from where the other

Rangers were, way off in the distance. He just laughed and said, "You idiot." Indeed. Taking a stroll like that by myself was pretty damn stupid, although I had Breston with me, which probably made me braver than it did smarter.

Breston and I didn't do much after that during that deployment. It presented a good opportunity to get out there and just get back on the horse as they say. In all, it took nine months from when my femurs shattered to return on missions with the boys. Never in a million years would I have thought that life would lead me down that path, but all the challenges I overcame and lessons I learned as a child combined to help get me there. I wasn't about to turn my back on that. It all came down to belief. Believe in yourself. It's truly amazing what the human mind can overcome.

We would catch a rotator back to Virginia Beach at the end of February/early March. I greeted my wife, who was happy to have me back, and of course, it made me happy to see my son who had been born a year earlier. I would begin a new workup at SEAL Team ▆ with a different dog soon so that I could redeploy to Afghanistan again in 2010.

With all that going on, I found out that my fireball of a daughter, Emma, would be born in November of 2009. When my son came into the world, he was just a quiet baby. An easy baby is what people would say. We needed that calmness at the time, and I think God knew we did. My daughter came into this world kicking and screaming—along with some piss and vinegar. Knowing her personality and talkative self at twelve years old now as I write this, I can certainly say I understand why she was that kind of baby. It was like she knew what she wanted but lacked the mobility and words to be able to communicate it. Both of my children are equally special in their own personalities. It's not easy leaving my family for deployment, and I credit Erica for holding down the fort when I had to leave.

CHAPTER 12

NO SUCCESS WITHOUT LOSSES

In May of 2010, I deployed with two new dogs: Rex and Tigo. Breston had returned to his squadron. I used Rex as the main dog and Tigo as an alternate in case Rex or another dog didn't work out—or worse, something happened to them. As great as Digo and Breston performed, things didn't always work out with every dog. Shit happens on the battlefield. Animals, like people, are unpredictable. You think you've done all you can, but then you get thrown a curveball.

Rex looked like a half-Malinois/half-shepherd mix. A serious dog. Sometimes, before deployment, I questioned whether he had the mental stability to properly do what we needed him to do. He would pass all the training exercises and then some, but every so often, he would just have this sideways-ass look that concerned me. However, never did I think he would endanger the team.

We deployed to FOB Shank, Afghanistan, in Logar Province. I absolutely hated that place. The bad guys would shoot two mortar rounds twice a day. We'd hear whistling and then an explosion. It absolutely sucked.

One day, outside the little PX (the military store on base), a mortar round came in. I had just left the PX and was on my way to our ATV for a ride back to the compound. The round hit right nearby. One of the military members that I didn't know took some shrapnel to his leg. I proceeded to help him until more military personnel showed up to render assistance. At that point, I handed someone his ID and let them take over. That happened in broad daylight when I should have been at my compound sleeping to rest for night missions. So there I was, taking fire on a store run. Might as well have been out on a mission. At least that way I could have had some control as the enemy fired at us.

For the most part, we just felt helpless when the sirens began and tried to make it to the designated bunker. Toward the end, I grew tired of getting out of my rack midday, so there were times I was just like, *Screw it. If I die, I die.* I'd lay my head down again and go back to sleep. No point in trying to run to the barriers that they had set up for shelter. If my number had come up, then so be it.

A few days later, a mortar round hit our compound wall and gym. The enemy would work those mortar shells around until they eventually hit what they wanted to hit. We found it nerve-racking to hear that whistling of the round and then just wait for it to land. I felt helpless sitting there like a duck, waiting to get nailed by one of those things.

That deployment presented several challenges, some of my own doing and some not. For starters, I was with a new troop because the troop I was accustomed to working with had to be split up all over various places. I found this new troop to be a tougher group. A lot of the guys were cool with support people, but others were difficult to figure out. Using the dog wasn't a huge priority on their list, but I would be ready when called up. That's all I could do at the time.

I had never gone on a deployment without a proven dog. Digo worked with his new handler, and I had not one but two new dogs. I took that challenge on because as a seasoned handler, I had confidence that I could do it. I got what I wished for, as that deployment had challenges from the beginning. We started a new camp at a different FOB and began with a blank slate. When we landed, we only had a few tents put up with no walls. We had to build everything out, but like always, we had everything we needed to make do.

I went out on a couple operations with Rex, and overall, we didn't have too much excitement. On one mission, our troop partnered with the Rangers. They would take one building or compound, and we would take the other. We thought that all the action would happen on the compound we targeted, but for the most part, that didn't happen. Command also forced us to go out with the Afghan Partner Unit, made up of Afghanis who, for the most part, just wanted to serve their country. I felt bad for them because it seemed like they had sent in a bunch of cats to do a dog's job, and believe me, it was like herding cats.

We sent the dog in first, and then the Afghani partner unit went in. Rex nailed a guy hiding upstairs. In my best voice, I told the Afghanis to let me take the dog off. They looked mortified by the dog's action; I think they had never seen a dog go after a guy like that before. Surprisingly, as bad as it looked, Rex had a mouthful of clothing and didn't do too much to the guy himself. It was rather thick material, so Rex's puncture wounds were not bad at all. Sometimes, when those dogs grabbed the person's clothes instead of getting a full mouth of human flesh, it made for a humorous time watching the person get dragged around the floor.

The neighboring compound presented a worse case. For some reason, the bad guys on that target had left the lights on. Turns out they had a reason. With the lights still burning, they could easily see the Rangers coming in. As soon as the Rangers broke into the courtyard, the enemy lit them up with gunfire. The Rangers took at least two casualties that night.

To make matters worse, they had issues sending their dog in deep. By that, I mean all the way in. In the dark, some dogs would have problems searching further into the compounds. Sometimes, they would hit a wall, thinking they had reached the end.

██████████████████████████████████ I once acted as a decoy in training. I sat in the dark, waiting for one of these revved-up beasts to come charging in. Having been on the receiving end of a charge in the dark, I can tell you that these dogs are moving so fast it's almost impossible to discern where they are in the room until they are right on you. ██

██

The cruel and harsh reality is that I'll always have the dog take a bullet over seeing one of the boys take a round. It's a risk we accept. I won't deny for one second that it isn't incredibly sad to lose a dog, but at the end of the day, they are a tool, and they are there for a purpose. I loved all my dogs, but I've seen enough funerals and little boys and girls having to grow up without their dads that I know I'm right.

With all the commotion at the Ranger compound, we received a call to send Rex and the team over to that building and begin clearing. Rex went into the courtyard and ran right into the building. As he began to clear, I could see ████████ that he was onto something. He beelined up the stairs and nailed a guy on the landing. While he handled that, the rest of our guys cleared the rest of the structure. One of the assaulters made it up to where Rex continued fighting the bad guy, who had been injured by a previous engagement with the Ranger, and saw he had an AK-47 right on him. So the assaulter put two rounds into the bad guy's head.

Rex continued to fight until I choked him off. Then, I quickly let Rex go and was gathering up my three-foot tether when he went back in for more. Brain matter and blood covered the dog as he proceeded to grab the guy by the head. He did an amazing job that night and made me proud. As awesome as the mission turned out, the loss of two Rangers deeply saddened us. I didn't know them, but it doesn't matter. Anytime I went out with them, I considered them my brothers.

I can only summarize the next mission as *shit happens*. We wanted every mission to turn out a success, but as hard as we trained, nothing was ever certain.

On that night's mission, we landed about two hundred meters from the objective. As soon as we landed, we heard reports of a squirter. One man had run off target, and I knew we had a chance to go hunt him down, but first, we used Rex to search several structures with no luck. We then went to hunt down the squirter. Up until this point, Rex had never—and I mean never—targeted one of the good guys.

The squirter had run off and hidden under a tree. We got in a line, and the call was made to send out the dog. We sent Rex out several times, thinking that he would nail the guy. An easy target. However, for some reason, he stopped, looked to our right flank, and appeared to target one of our guys on the end. Rex took off, and I immediately started to call him off, but he had reached our guy before I could finish the words. Meanwhile, we stood exposed in a field flanked by buildings. Rex had fully committed. I had honestly never seen anything like it. I had to physically remove him from my own teammate. Rex had injured him pretty bad, and man, it just sucked.

I pressed on with the team, thinking the incident was only a fluke. However, at one point, while sending Rex out, he caught wind of our interpreter, sensing him as a threat, and went after him. It seemed like firing a bullet without aiming. I didn't quite understand it, and it absolutely defeated me inside. The interpreter ended up okay, and we continued to pursue that one asshole. I kept thinking if I had Digo, that wouldn't have been an issue.

We eventually caught up with the squirter. Time for lights out. Since we could see the guy and recognized that he wouldn't cooperate, we decided to send Rex. Third time's the charm, right? Nope, not even close. I literally keyed Rex up on the target guy, and I know to this day Rex saw him. So I sent Rex. He went out ten feet, turned around, and nailed one of our guys on the bicep. Right then and there, I fired him. I made up my mind that Rex would never go out in the field again, at least not with me. Sure enough, we never used him after that.

On the way back, people could see that I was upset. I'd never expected my own dog to do something like that. I had spent a good three years building my great reputation, and Rex had tarnished it in one operation. It was especially bad because it had happened with a troop I didn't usually work with as opposed to the one that knew my track record. So much for a first impression.

Overall, no one gave a damn, and they all forgave me. The civilian trainer took Rex back to the command after that operation. I took that as a huge learning moment, and instead of letting it consume me, I decided to use it as motivation to do better next time. Rex would eventually go off to a police department. Most of the departments, except for SWAT, did not need the complexity of searching with multiple teammates. Rex could bite, and he did well with his new handler.

Tigo was not Rex. Tigo, a Belgian Malinois, had an obsessive-compulsive disorder with licking the door of a crate. I found it absolutely remarkable and gross at the same time. He'd leave foam on the door like a rabid dog, but Tigo didn't have rabies. I could trust Tigo to lay in the hooch and not piss, crap, or tear anything up. Although smaller than Rex, he had Digo's size. Tigo, a quiet dog, worked with absolute stealth. He did have one minor flaw though— chickens. Chickens absolutely freaked him out. I remember the first time we went out on target with him, we noticed a bunch of farm animals on the ████████████████████████████████████ I didn't think anything of it because I never thought we'd have an issue. I'd never had a dog that was scared of other animals. We trained around them from time to time. Maybe only Afghan chickens freaked him out. Kidding, of course.

Tigo and I patrolled in with our assigned team. It was a pretty easy hump in because that part of Afghanistan had relatively flat terrain. I remember a lot of my walks in. My favorite thing in the world, enjoying those peaceful nights. A good business idea could involve setting up a training village somewhere in the States and taking people on a patrol into a target with role players. I would pay money just to walk back on a Chinook and feel the exhaust blast from the engine. It's a whole other type of adrenaline. People would pay huge bucks to do stuff like that. They could kit up with NODs, SIM guns with lasers, all the other gear for a fun experience. Maybe include the dogs as well. A different kind of dog therapy.

Tigo and I moved forward side by side, enjoying the brisk, Afghan night. Far too many stars to count in that beautiful night sky. It reminded me of parts of Texas at night. Once we reached the ORP, I got Tigo's vest ready. I made all my dogs patrol with it on. Some handlers carried it for the dog because people thought it would make the dog tired. I never believed that because once dogs became keyed up for a search, nothing could stop them, especially a Malinois. They would work until they died.

We conducted a callout on the target building. As usual, the compound had huge walls. I opted to wait for someone to open a door rather than crawl over a huge-ass wall. I'd done it before, but if I didn't have to, I wouldn't. Fortunately, the door stayed propped open after the men, women, and children came out. At that point, I sent Tigo in, and he immediately began to search, clearing multiple structures without me seeing anyone inside and without him finding anyone. Then, he came to the courtyard, where he encountered a chicken. He began hopping around, barking at it like *what the hell is that goofy-looking thing?* I'm not sure if the combination of the night and never having seen a chicken before spooked Tigo or what.

The next time we went out, we had a little more action for Tigo. We patrolled like normal to our ORP where I prepared the dog. Again, we faced large walls, so I opted for someone to open the door. After the call, Tigo went in to search for anyone remaining or for any explosives still inside. He began to search the compound room by room, and we pushed him further and further. Eventually, Tigo flowed into one room where he began to circle over and over and throw his head up toward the ceiling. He had a scent and began to act more frantic. That alarmed me a bit because I knew he had sensed a human odor, but we couldn't see him or her ██████████

Tigo eventually reached a bed where he encountered a man and began to bite him on the leg and torso. Compared to other dogs I'd worked with, Tigo didn't have the nastiest bite in the world. He kind of just held onto the guy and shook him a bit. I've seen dogs that would tear a calf or a forearm muscle straight from the bone. There's no coming back from that either. But Tigo had a different style.

At that point, I called Tigo off, and he came back down the stairs. I would yell the command "Heir" and then give him a vibrate on the electronic collar so that he understood a correction would come if he didn't obey. I didn't like that method, but we needed to give everyone the opportunity to give up. That was the new way of doing things. It really sucked, and I believe policies developed by people who don't actually do the fighting—or work for that matter—can make a job really difficult or dangerous. We indeed were trying to win the hearts and minds by doing things that way, but if you've been given every chance to come out, I feel like you're fair game.

We called for the guy to come out, but he refused. In response, we said we would send the dog back in, something I always wanted. I really enjoyed free bites. So did the dogs, I'm sure. Almost immediately after we said that, the guy emerged, hands up and willing to do damn near anything we wanted him to do. That operation went really well, and even more, it worked out well for me and Tigo. A fantastic win.

A couple of missions later, we had an awesome operation that I was looking forward to. We had bad guys on target who had multiple weapons, and I just knew that the team would use the dog. In Afghanistan, for the most part, the enemy fought us. In Iraq, they simply blew shit up. Chickenshit bitches in Iraq. They would pretty much set off an IED or camp in corners worse than people who play *Call of Duty*. Afghanistan seemed fair in my eyes—well, to a point. At least they used guns.

We patrolled in, and again, I reveled in my time with Tigo, enjoying that peaceful walk under the stars. Peace before the crap hit the fan, that is. Tigo and I met with our team at the ORP. Sometimes we rolled with the RECCE guys up front, and sometimes we rolled with the team or even in the rear with the command and control (C2) element. I didn't particularly like that because I felt it was smarter for the dog to lead. We never knew who lay in wait for us during the walk-in, and I knew the dog might discover them before bad things happened.

At the ORP, I set up Tigo's vest and met with my team. After we entered the compound, we were met with an exchange of fire. We killed one bad guy

in a window and engaged another in the courtyard. We then sent Tigo in to search. Immediately, Tigo charged up the stairs and engaged the guy we had shot through the window. ▮▮▮▮▮▮▮▮▮▮▮▮▮▮▮▮▮▮
▮▮▮▮ The rest of the team flowed in while I pulled Tigo off. Next, I sent Tigo into the courtyard, where he rolled past the other body and continued through the target until the team announced it secure.

Over the radio, we heard that we had a follow-on target that would require us to go to a different building. A follow-on target develops from the different ways we track them. I'm not at liberty to say how we track them, but the bad guys likely know how we find them. I went with the team to the follow-on target, joining my favorite team leader with that troop. I found him to be both understanding and chill. Upon arriving at the building, we immediately engaged one guy on the balcony. When we sent Tigo in, he searched like a damn champ. To get him in there, I climbed a ladder with him and sent him down the stairs from the roof. He then reached a stairway and started barking at the ceiling. Though he was indicating a guy at that location, I could not see a door or anything. Well, immediately to the right was a small door that led to the animal coop. Little did I know that a guy lurked in there, waiting for us with a fully loaded AK.

I proceeded to tell my team leader that Tigo had a man's odor, and he couldn't get to the guy. He kept searching though, so I continued to work my way across the roof until I came within about ten feet of Tigo. I could see the guy on the balcony room that we had shot, and I put two more in him to make sure he was not just lying there. Then, I guided Tigo back to the stairs that I'd come up with a red overt laser, at which point I scooped him up.

Next, we sent in the Afghan Partner Unit, and they continued to clear up to that door. As soon as they broke the threshold, the guy inside lit up the doorway. We happened to be on the same roof that the guy sat under. Out of nowhere, rounds came shooting through. Like a damn cheetah, I grabbed Tigo and leapt to the roof next to us. Eventually, they killed the guy inside, then called me and Tigo back to finish working the target. So we sent him from the roof into the second-story rooms. He hit the dead guy from when we first rolled up on target and continued to work until he finished securing the target. Tigo did absolutely amazing, and I couldn't have been prouder of that pup.

Resilience is everything in the world. Nothing will go perfectly, as evidenced by the things that happened at the start of my deployment. It made me absolutely miserable. I worked with a new troop I didn't really know or have a connection with. The guys in the troop I had worked with when I had my injury in Iraq accepted me for who I was, an MA, not a SEAL, but one trying to do everything I could to help them. I had a different experience with the troop on that later deployment. They seemed tight knit, and whether I liked it or not, they constantly reminded me that I wasn't really one of them. I knew in my heart that they needed the dog, and I would do everything I could to make sure I inserted that dog to protect them.

My first deployment in Iraq taught me the incredible value of these dogs. I saw that again in my return deployment in 2009 with Breston and recognized how vital a dog could be in determining success. Don't get me wrong, those guys could probably accomplish all they wanted without the dog, but to me, if my dog's life spared one of my brothers, then I would use him every time. At the end of the day, the dog is there so that the team can come home.

Looking back at that deployment, the ability to overcome huge obstacles played a role in me overcoming my epic screwup with Rex. In fact, it was a lesson I'd been learning most of my life. I remember as a kid getting suspended from school for doing something stupid—I should've known better. Then, when I watched my dad go off to prison, and even when I joined the guard and then "quit" at seventeen, I overcame. I didn't let any of those things define me, and I sure as hell wasn't going to let that mess-up with Rex destroy me.

It's important we remind ourselves that we are not defined by one mistake or accomplishment but rather what we do as a whole in life. It's about where we are now and how we got there through all the success and all the failure. We absolutely can't have wins in life without taking some losses. I would rather fail nine out of ten times and have one great success than give up and never try. I think that is where we fail our youth. We don't let them fail. We give them trophies or simply push them through school instead of letting them fail and then explaining to them why they didn't do well and how they need to do better in order to succeed.

I learned so much on that mission. Knock me down, and I'll get right back up.

CHAPTER 13
THE DUTCH SHEPHERD

O ne Thanksgiving, I thought about what I was thankful for. The working dogs I had partnered with certainly came to mind. Without them, my story would have turned out far different. It would be less exciting and, perhaps most of all, not nearly as fulfilling. Most importantly, I'm thankful for the countless number of times they called upon those dogs to do things that we simply could not do without them—or at least without the level of success that we had.

I didn't select Brando myself. A group of the SEAL teams trainers selected him for training at our kennel. They put the dogs through the same rigorous testing that many dogs before them had gone through. Just as many fine sailors don't make it past BUD/S and many fine SEALs don't make it to SEAL Team ▮, not all dogs make it. Only the best of the best. And when I say rigorous, I mean it. They'd put the dogs on helicopters, planes, and boats. They'd use hellish gunfire, door breaching, and flash grenades. We'd throw them in a boat and expect them to do over the beach (OTB) training where they would have to swim a few hundred meters.

Soon after Brando finished his portion of the selection and training, I asked kennel leadership to pair me with him—a Dutch shepherd the size of a damn horse. Brando had the personality of a dog you could have around your family and children but also had the switch to turn on his dark side at game time. I absolutely loved that dog for those reasons.

Don't confuse Brando with Digo. Digo was Satan incarnate. That dog would bite you if you stopped petting him. He certainly had some screws loose but for sure did his job, and that's why I loved Digo. On the other hand, Brando seemed to have his screws somewhat tightened. When they paired me up with Brando at the end of 2010 for my June deployment, I knew he would become something special. Brando would not only play a role in protecting the team but also in helping me to heal in the aftermath of Extortion 17 and the loss of all the men in that helicopter crash. The year 2011 proved to be one of the deadliest of the war for U.S. forces.

I remember the first time I brought Brando up to the guys in the team room. A few of them really took to him. They first asked me if he was friendly. I replied that I'd trust this dog with my kids and wife, so yes, friendly indeed. As I began to bring him around One Troop (my troop assignment), they came to trust him more and more. We did a lot of house runs with Brando, meaning we'd line up in the stack and clear houses room by room. That's basic as I can be about house runs, and much more goes into it, but I'm not at liberty to share that. The first time, Brando and I lined up about three or four men deep as we patrolled into this complex of concrete buildings. As Brando and I practiced, he just knew his position.

We had role players in the buildings to make it as realistic as possible. We ran with paint and fake crash body simulators, and of course, Brando wore a standard Ray Allen leather muzzle. We surrounded the first building, and Brando and I waited for our turn. We wouldn't have to wait long.

The team wanted to hit the first building silently, so it was important for the dog to remain absolutely quiet. It is extremely hard to keep a dog quiet, which is why we always trained the dogs to move stealthily. They were only allowed to bark when the explosives or breaching went off. Additionally, we trained the dogs to bark on command so that when the interpreters told the people in the buildings to come out or the dogs would come in, they could believe us.

Brando obeyed and was at the ready as the assaulters quietly woke people up. We stayed in the stack until about the second floor where a role player fired off blank rounds toward the stairwell. We had created that war game for the dogs. They could now run freely because the bad guys knew we had arrived, and we no longer had the element of surprise.

The team leader called for the dog.

"Dog up," I said.

The team leader replied, "Send it."

That always excited me. Whether training or on target, I always found it fun to send the dogs. I watched a YouTuber, Larry Enticer, doing a lot of crazy stuff and will just say, "I'm just gonna send it," or "I'm still gonna send it." I'd like to think his expression mirrors that of mine when we released the hounds.

On his first search, Brando encountered the guy firing the blanks and started muzzle striking him as he lay on the floor. I got Brando off of him before too many hits. We continued to search the rest of the building, constantly sending Brando into one room after another. Finally, building secure. We then had a follow-on building to hit (again, just training). We moved to cover around that building and started to call out the people. A couple came out and then one last call followed by the command "dog up." We chucked a fake crash body at that doorway and with my red laser, I pointed at the doorway, and the dog followed it in. Immediately, I ███████████ called out that we had two people fighting the dog, and they made the call to move up and start clearing.

I called Brando off, and while the assaulters wrapped those guys up, I checked to make sure his muzzle remained secure. Those training fights could get intense, and I didn't need an accidental bite. After confirming his muzzle was still on, I shouted "dog up" at the foot of the stairwell. Brando charged up and proceeded to continue to clear.

Brando reached the last door and began barking while another call came over the radio indicating that a squirter had fled from a different building into the woods, a typical scenario that happened all the time. I informed the team that the dog had found someone behind the door, although I obviously couldn't see anyone. The dogs were trained to bark when they found inaccessible people. They would bark and hold on the door or try their damnedest to get in. One assaulter popped the door open, and Brando went tearing inside. Sure enough, a guy stood in the room, and Brando hit him, bringing him to the floor and going after him over and over.

With that building secure, the next task involved going after the squirter. Squirters presented a tailor-made situation for using the dogs, so I moved to the exterior and met up with three or four assaulters, at which point I unmuzzled the dog. Then, I gave Brando the rolling R command to search. As he moved side to side out in front of us, we could see him go really fast and then slow right down as he settled in on a scent. Once he tracked the squirter down, Brando took off and grabbed the guy, who smartly wore a bite suit.

With the training exercise over, I felt damn good. It was a huge win for a first time out with Brando and the guys, even if only training. I found him to be truly a great dog.

In training, we had practiced fast roping, which essentially meant sliding down a rope from a hovering helicopter for a quick infil. The dog and I had to go either first or last because we had a device we hooked up that helped us descend at a reasonable rate. It used the friction of the rope and worked well unless put on upside down. In that case, we'd fly to the ground. Smack! I could not imagine hooking my dog to me and trying to control fast roping down using only my hands and legs. I could do it but would have an extra eighty pounds of dog on top of me.

I never, ever wanted to be last, so I made it a goal to convince my troop chief to let us go first out of one side of the helicopter while the team started out the other side. I would much rather sit at the back of the ramp on the right side so that I could swing out and then face the helicopter as I went down. We wanted to descend as fast as possible, and as soon as my feet hit the ground, I wanted to be ready at the bottom to pull that quick release. If I wasn't fast enough, chances were another guy would slide down right on top of me. I had a harness that went from myself to the dog and then from the middle of that harness to the device itself. I usually don't trust things too much, but our equipment was pretty highly rated, and all the gear we had worked for climbing. We arrived at the helicopter as that exhaust I enjoyed hit my face and walked in the back of the CH-47 Chinook.

The Chinook took off and hovered at twenty feet. Brando and I were clipped to each other with a lanyard attached to a rope that popped the lanyard. I made sure to keep the device high and out of the way. We swung out, and just like that, we lowered to the ground. Once there, I grabbed the device and pulled it down as far as I could so people coming down wouldn't hit it. Flawless.

I should have stopped at one, but I was like, *Screw it—let's do another repetition,* and the Chinook crew obliged. So following the same procedure, we clipped in and swung out. I immediately knew something was wrong. Brando and I fell twenty feet to the ground. We were holding the rope, but there was no tension. I landed on my back, and Brando looked at me like *what the hell.* Luckily, we had no injuries.

Once the helicopter cut the ropes, I looked at the device. I had connected it correctly, but I'm sure when I swung out, I didn't have enough tension on the device and the rope. That caused me to drop like a brick, but we're lucky nothing else happened. After that, I said, "To hell with that—I'm not doing another. I've got a whole deployment to get through."

———

June of 2011 came, and that meant time for deployment. At the time, my son was three years old, and my daughter was two years old. I knew I neared the point of being done as my body was really starting to give out. I had experienced a lot of what I would call micro-concussions. I don't know if that's a thing, but every time I was near a door breach or didn't have hearing protection during gunfire, it felt like my brain would lock up for a second, and then I would remember where I was.

Extortion 17 happened on that deployment. A life-altering moment that still doesn't feel real. Even to this day, I catch myself wanting to call John Douangdara, whom I called Jet. We called him by his nickname, Jet Li, or Jet for short. He enlisted in the U.S. Navy in February of 2003, and the navy selected him for SEAL Team ███ in 2008 following his service at two other navy commands. Jet's competence for the job, I think, is why they selected him.

Back at the command, when I first met him after my return to the unit from rehabilitation, I walked up to the kennel, looking forward to meeting Jet.

He approached me with a big smile and said, "I'm here to take your place."

I always remember that smile because many noticed it as one of his greatest qualities. That and his incredible loyalty and friendship.

Jet immediately became the brother that I never had. I built so many great memories with him both stateside and overseas. Over the next three years, we deepened that brotherly relationship. We would train every day together because we served in the same squadron and did just about everything together. I would say that he became one of my closest friends, especially during that deployment in Afghanistan. We would talk all the time on the phone because he worked down south, and I was up north. We had so much in common. I miss him and miss all those who perished.

That would be my only tour with Brando, and also my final deployment. Brando would go on to deploy several more times, but with a different handler. During this deployment, I went to Jalalabad, Afghanistan, for the first time. I heard about some of the hikes to target, and they sounded gnarly. That area had daunting, mountainous terrain, but I'd done it before. I had a healthy and solid dog. A truly badass dog.

One of the first missions gave Brando his first bite. I examined the mission planning, taking in what the buildings looked like, the flight in, and the patrol in. I always prepared because I needed to know how much water to bring the dog, how long I'd be walking, and if we expected any obstacles. I also wanted to know where I could best position the dog for the assault on the target and in case we had squirters. I would always kit up the dog first. Only once I was sure he had everything would I make sure my kit was tight.

I always re-jammed my magazines after every op and got our kit set up and ready to go for the next one. We never knew when they'd call us to go out, so I wanted us to be as prepared as possible beforehand. As usual, I put on Brando's non-ballistic vest, the best choice if he needed to be light and maneuverable. ████████████████████████████████████

██

I put on my CRYE Precision MultiCam kit, Salomons, helmet, and NODs, then grabbed my little pea-shootin' MP7 with forty-round magazines and suppressor. A light weapon, but I had snipers and other SEALs with me who loved to shoot for a living and carried some serious hardware. Bottom line, if it came down to my little MP7, then shit had gotten real, and life was sucking.

I carried extra MP7 magazines in addition to my standard loadout, but I also carried four extra M4 magazines that I could give to the guys if we really got into it. We just never knew what kind of stuff we might stir up on the ops we went on. Kinda like taking down an abandoned beehive in a tree, thinking it's empty, but nestled inside is a whole colony. We'd think that there were only four bad guys on target, and then out of nowhere, dudes would come creeping out of every nook and cranny like roaches. Luckily, I had a badass dog as my weapon.

Next, we went to the buses where they took a headcount before taking us to the airfield. Once there, we waited for the signal from the helicopter crew to come aboard. As usual, I put an earbud into one ear and listened to some of my favorite music. I played one song in particular quite a lot: "Down with the Sickness" by Disturbed. That song always put me in the mood. I loved another chance to walk to the helicopter with the heat and exhaust from the engines just blasting as we boarded. It felt good. I then took my seat toward the middle of the helicopter and put Brando between my legs so no one would step on him. The bird lifted off, and we went on our way for yet another mission.

We landed in this little field and spread out, waiting for the helicopter to lift off. It was amazing. I was back in Afghanistan, doing what I loved. I had two rods in my femurs, but all that hard work in rehab had really paid off in the end. If I hadn't busted my ass, I wouldn't have been on my third deployment after the explosion. After my deployment with Breston, Rex, and Tigo, I had the confidence built back up that I could keep doing this.

We patrolled to the target building, and on the way there, I let Brando roam off leash, but he was in my sight at all times. We wanted the dogs out searching in front in case they found explosives or people. I enjoyed watching him work. As we walked, I started to smell something. I hadn't smelled that certain scent since high school. Well, by damn, we were walking through a field of marijuana. No, I didn't take any, but once you smell pot, you remember it.

Through the fields, we walked, and we received word that several people had squirted from the building and run up in the hills, maneuvering with weapons. They had too much of a head start, so we let them go and called in air support to take care of them.

From there, we continued to the building where we called on anyone inside to come out. They already knew we had arrived, so there was no point in trying to be stealthy. Twelve people started to emerge. A couple of men but a lot of women and girls.

Meanwhile, two more guys with AK-47s began working to get in position to hit us, but we already had people set up on the corners who quickly engaged them. Two bad guys down. Next, we sent Brando in to ensure they weren't playing possum. As he moved up, I continued to say *stellen* over and over again so he would engage. At first, he only sniffed because we used clothing in training that had man scent on it. It became a bridge to getting a real bite. Sure enough, after a moment, Brando grabbed a mouthful of human, and I let him have at it for a few seconds before calling him off.

Satisfied that we had secured the situation around the building, we moved inside, sending Brando in to search room by room for any other hostiles. When he reached one room, he started acting like he had a man odor. Sure enough, one guy had stayed in the building, and Brando immediately started to bite and engage him. I told the team, and they proceeded to move in with me right behind.

I told Brando to continue biting: "*Stellen*, Brando, *stellen*." For encouragement, I also told him *brave hond* (good dog in Dutch). I spoke Dutch to him because Brando had come from the Netherlands.

Brando kept at the guy, but he didn't thrash like Digo, so he created a bite wound that was a lot cleaner with a lot less blood. Finally, satisfied the guy no longer posed a threat, I called off Brando, and the guys rolled up another military-age male (MAM).

We searched the rest of the buildings with Brando leading the way. Target secured. With that, we patrolled back out into the fields we'd seen earlier for exfil. The ride home in the helicopter was like a glorious sleep you only experience once in a blue moon. I fell asleep hard. It had been a highly successful mission with Brando doing a great job. So satisfying. As Ice Cube would say, "It was a good day."

In August 2011, we experienced the tragedy of Extortion 17, the largest loss of life in Naval Special Warfare history since the start of the conflicts in Iraq and Afghanistan after 9/11. On that night, August 6, 2011, thirty American servicemen and a dog would go out and not come home. We lost thirty-one irreplaceable heroes. Families would soon learn of the fate of those men and the dog. They were part of a quick reaction force, and my friend, Jet Li, was on board with his dog, Bart. A random rocket-propelled grenade RPG shot down their helicopter (call sign Extortion 17) as they flew toward a mission to do what they loved. The RPG hit one of the rotors, sending the helicopter crashing violently to the ground.

I've waited a while to write about this story in detail because I slip off into a dark place when I think about it, and I have to claw my way out of a hole. The brain is such a powerful tool. When we remember traumatic experiences, all of our senses are heightened, but sometimes, it seems to have incremental growth. I think the thing with PTSD is that it will never go away. I will never *not* have that sad feeling, but I've learned to deal with the sadness by remembering the good times.

I would do anything to be able to tell Jet that he was like a part of our family. He once came to my home, we assumed to chat with us, but we found him just sitting there, feeding my baby son Cheerios. He spent time with us often and even helped us move into our first home. Simply put, he was family.

When I spoke to him that night, he talked about how he could rile up our program manager because he liked messing with him, and I think the retired master chief, who had brought us both to the command, knew he did. Jet would also take my ID, put it in water, and throw it in the freezer. Then, I'd get him back by screwing with this little Buddha figure in his car. All fun and games. Jet liked to play around like that. That's what I loved about him. He never had a negative attitude and simply had one of those personalities that drew people toward him. His dog, Bart, was a spaz, and I think they both complemented each other. I'm so grateful to have met him.

Prior to getting off the phone that night, he said they thought they were spinning up on something, and like always, I said, "Stay safe, brother. I love ya, bro."

That night, after I finished working out for what seemed like the hundredth time, I sat in my room watching *Family Guy* because it was the only thing I could find at the time. It took me away from the monotonous grind of being on deployment when we weren't going out on target that day. I also stayed busy taking online college classes. I'd go on a mission and endure a large gun battle. Then, two hours later, I'd hop online to engage in discussion posts for the classes. That evening, at the same time, I also had my wife on Skype, and we chatted away. One of my teammates walked in the room and said to turn on the channel where we could watch different targets and ongoing missions. I quickly logged off with my wife. I believe she knew something bad had happened since I did not return the call until several hours later.

When I clicked on the channel, I could see a big ball of fire and what looked like a helicopter. My throat sank to my stomach.

I asked, already knowing the answer. "Are those our guys?"

"Yes."

What else could he say?

"Where's the second bird?" I asked, knowing that another had flown with Extortion 17.

He shook his head. "It didn't get hit."

He went on to say that he thought everyone had died. A fully loaded helicopter. I just couldn't fathom it, and I kept asking why. I had so many questions. For some time, I just remember watching that screen over and over. I could see secondary explosions going off from what I presume were grenades detonating as a result of the heat and the burning of the helicopter. I only hoped that they went quickly because no one could get in that helicopter to save them as hot as it burned. It seemed like it burned for two days.

A while later, I called my wife and asked her to leave Chicago where she had been staying with her parents and go to Virginia Beach where most of the families lived because they'd soon be overwhelmed. It was then I had to tell her Jet would not be coming home.

It was just so damn sad and miserable. I drank so much alcohol just to try to get rid of the feeling. As I watched the footage of the Army Rangers pulling out bodies and equipment from the helicopter, I remember thinking how easily I could take my MP7 weapon and put myself out of my misery. I literally sat in the dog kennel with the gun pressed to my chin. However, I'd abruptly have to shift the task at hand. Next, it would be our turn to go and pack up all their belongings at FOB Shank.

I arrived at what seemed like a ghost town. The tents felt eerie. Nothing seemed right. I sat down at Jet's desk and put on his headphones to see what he had last listened to. I don't remember what it was, but it was the type of music Jet had enjoyed. We then began to pack up their stuff. Little by little, we loaded up their portable storage containers, a difficult thing to do.

The hardest part came next. The body bags that they'd loaded didn't just hold bodies. They were filled with guns, kits, and other things. The smell of burnt flesh lingered on the equipment, and bag by bag, we tried to identify weapons based on serial numbers. It's a smell I'll never forget. Ever. Meticulously, we went through it all until we were finished.

The Ranger dog handler asked if I wanted to hear how they'd found Jet and Bart. I think I felt so numb at the time that I figured I couldn't hear anything worse than what I had already seen—that is, until he told me the next part. They'd found Jet and his dog almost fused together; it looked like he had been holding Bart. That made me think that they had suffered in the end. I'll never know what happened, but Jet's love for that dog showed all the way.

The ramp ceremony, the final step in sending them home, came next. They also draped seven Afghan flags on caskets for those whose remains we couldn't identify—the seven Afghanis that flew on the helicopter. That seemed like utter bullshit, but what did I know at that moment? I'm not some five-star general or admiral, and I didn't make those decisions. I didn't fly back with them; rather, we had to stay and finish out the deployment.

Even still, I feel like I've never had true closure. We sent them home, but I never really had the chance to emotionally close that chapter. Years later, I've come to terms with what happened. An RPG with a lucky shot took out thirty-one heroes. The guy who was responsible boasted and bragged and headed for Pakistan expecting to receive a hero's welcome. Instead, we met him with a missile. Sent to go see his seventy-two virgins. Screw that guy. Screw 'em all.

Writing those sentences felt like a gut punch. My injury and the uncertainty were tough. I had prepared to accept the outcome and could handle both the physical and mental aspects. I could take that. However, I could not take the mass casualty and all those brothers dying. Losing so many people I knew, whether close friends or not, became one of the most difficult things I had ever faced. I had interacted with all those guys at some point with the dogs, so it brought me to a breaking point.

I would love to say it gets easier to talk about, but it doesn't. All I can do, all I attempt to do every day, is be sure that I'm doing the things that they would have wanted me to do. I know that sounds like a platitude, but that's the best way I can honor their memory. We put those boys and Bart the dog on the plane destined for their final resting places, and that was it. No more training exercises with them, no more sitting at a dive bar in Miami talking about the dogs, nothing. No more of Jet's smile. Those days are over.

After a short time, I was definitely ready to get back after it. I needed to do something other than cry about losing all of those guys. I believe the higher-ups held us back from going out for a while because they wanted everyone to have a clear mind. However, in August 2011, we all wanted to get back out and tear stuff up after the tragedy of Extortion 17. Finally, they decided to send us after the people in the foothills of Tora Bora.

That could be fun, I thought.

Anytime we went out with One Troop, I knew they'd give the dog some action. I loved when they involved us over and over. It made me feel useful. I always wanted to keep proving my worth. Although I never endured BUD/S, wore the Trident, or made selection for ███████████████, I did have expertise in working with the dogs. Of course, when a dog messed up, I had to answer for it, but man, when we did great, did we ever get praised.

Like any other night, I geared up and went to the helicopters. I'm not going to lie, I thought about the guys as I rode on the aircraft. I had never thought about being shot down until Extortion 17 happened. However, I quickly shook off any fear because if it's your time, then it's your time. So I fell asleep waiting for the thirty-second-out call. I washed my mind of everything so that I could be clearheaded once we needed to handle things. As we rode in, I listened to Marilyn Manson's "The Beautiful People" on repeat.

At thirty seconds out, I pulled out my iPod radio earbud, put it away, and grabbed Brando's vest. When I did that, Brando knew it was game time. He was ready. I was ready. As I looked at the men around the aircraft,

I looked in awe at my family of crusaders of ███ Squadron and knew that I planned to have their back just like they would have mine. Thinking back on it, I consider that a true honor.

We landed, exited, and took up security as the helicopters unloaded and waited. We patrolled in, but as we started moving, we saw squirters running from the target. One idiot decided to go into a square patch of reeds. I planned to get his ass, but he'd have to wait. How crazy exciting to know without a doubt that your dog is going to get a bite? Once a dog has the fun of biting a man—a real man, not some decoy—they just seem to want it so bad. There's something about a grown man screaming like a little girl that you can't quite replicate in training. Dogs love that stuff. I loved that shit. Also, it helps when your dog can outweigh and out-tough guys who are smaller than him.

We patrolled in, and nothing crazy happened. We circled up just outside the target, and everyone got their ladders and other necessary items. Brando and I just waited. At the first courtyard, we conducted a callout. As we did that, one man ran with a weapon. I'm not sure exactly how, but they took him down about two hundred to three hundred meters from my location.

After everyone came out of the building, the call came over for the dog. We moved up to the first courtyard and sent Brando in. Although he searched his little heart out, he found nothing. While I was grateful for no barricaded shooters waiting for us, I knew that dogs were not 100 percent in finding someone. So in the back of my mind, I always wondered if Brando had missed anyone. We then moved in with the assault team, and I continued to send Brando before anyone else, even though he had already searched. After all, that wasn't a damn test. It wasn't training. I might as well try a few more times just to be sure, right?

After we secured that area, another team called me to link up with them. As we moved up, they said to send the dog because we sometimes had to assume some of the bad guys played possum as stated before. Brando left my side and made a beeline to the MAM who had been shot and lay on the ground. The dog started pulling him around like a ragdoll. Nope, no sign of life there, but damn good on him if he had been pretending and endured that from Brando without giving himself away.

Then, we moved past that guy for my gift still waiting in the square patch of field. Like how damn dumb do you have to be to hear aircraft above and hear a dog barking and to then basically run into a corner? I guess being scared of the boogeyman coming after you will do that.

I kept sending Brando. Nothing. I was like, *What the hell? This should be easy.* Well, it hadn't occurred to me that we stood upwind. I had focused so much on the dog that I forgot the basic principles of performing an open area search. My team leader, a prior SEAL dog handler, pointed that out to me. We repositioned downwind, and as soon as we did that, Brando caught the scent.

We had trained Brando with Afghan-worn clothes prior to deployment, so he knew what those guys smelled like. We legally purchased and used clothes from Afghanis that had been worn and never washed. For example, we often compensated prior detainees for their clothing that was so beat up and torn that they no longer wanted it. These clothes had the actual fear scent. The sweat that poured out from those guys when scared shitless had baked in those rags. Keep in mind, dogs smell fear because humans emit a particular scent when they're frightened.

Almost immediately, Brando locked onto the guy's scent. Being a nice guy, my team leader told the interpreter to give out one more warning that we planned to send the dog. No response. *Let's play.*

I gave Brando the *stellen* and rolling R command. *Go get your bite on.* Without hesitation, Brando leaped into the reeds, and a second later, we heard screaming. The team leader told me to call Brando off, so I did. We were unsure whether the guy had a gun or whatever he had planted in there, and we certainly didn't want to walk into a trap. I recalled Brando, and the team leader gave the guy another chance. We preferred to not pull his ass out, but again, he decided not to emerge. So we sent Brando back in. If the first bite wasn't a freebee, now we'd definitely have icing on the cake. I told Brando to *stellen*, and once I knew he had the guy, I started telling him to *apport*, which means retrieve. As if the bad guy were a big stick, Brando dragged his ass to the edge of the reeds. By that time, the guy had stopped messing around. I called Brando off of him so that my team could cuff the guy up. He was lucky. He could have been shot, but in the end, he chose life over full-on jihad.

After we finished and started walking back, I pulled a Coke out of my backpack. I always came with a frozen Coke because by the time we finished the op, I needed some caffeine. It always felt good to have a Coke after a good op, and it was also just something nice to drink on the way back out. Of course, I only did that after we had secured things and walked back to the middle of nowhere. I sure wasn't going to grab a drink while we operated in the middle of some city or village.

Some missions went like that. A peaceful walk-in. A nice bite for the dog. No casualties on our side. A nice walk back out and a cold Coke. Some missions, though, could get pretty spotty.

We had one mission close enough for us to drive in, and I put Brando in the back of a side-by-side with me. We had little protection, but I knew that I could dismount pretty quickly if needed. We drove about six kilometers through the city to a little town just outside of Jalalabad. People stared at us as we rolled through town, and we didn't know who was good and who was bad or who might be making phone calls to warn the enemy.

We had only one target building that night. Shortly after arriving, we received reports of people squirting out of one of the target buildings to a bunch of weeds and brush. At least I knew then and there that I would get the chance to run after squirters with Brando.

When we arrived at the vehicle drop-off point, we dismounted and set up rear security. We patrolled through the town about five hundred feet toward the target building. I stood in an alleyway with Brando attached to me by a small tether. I kept holding rear security, waiting for our turn to go in and help while they conducted a callout on the main building.

An announcement came over the radio that movers had been seen by the overhead asset coming toward us from another building. Then, a loud barrage of gunfire rang out about one hundred meters away from me down the alley, but I couldn't tell exactly where it came from. I immediately grabbed Brando by the vest and dodged behind another building to take cover. Our return fire exposed the enemy, causing them to take off toward another building. More gunfire came in my direction as rounds popped off a car and little puffs of dirt rose from the ground. A close call for me. Meanwhile, the enemy fighters escaped into a building we could not identify.

After we completed the callout, we decided to send Brando in so he could search for anyone who remained. However, we would soon find out that the people we looked for were actually the people who had squirted from the building. As Brando searched, the overhead asset could see the two individuals run off and hunker down. Having that in the back of my mind, I continued to clear until we secured the target. We found nothing in the target building.

After I linked up with the team that would go after the squirter, I sent Brando out into this soaking wet field. It reminded me of my first deployment with Digo when I fell into that shit field of water runoff. As we began working our way toward the squirter, I decided to walk on the built-up dirt that separated the fields. We worked our way down to knee-deep water, and I began to dry heave from the nasty smell. In the meantime, people were laughing and making fun of each other, all while we were looking for the bad guys. We always found something comical while out on a mission, even at the weirdest times.

After I made it past the dry heaves, I sent Brando out further and further until he began to lock onto something. I could see him working a cone of scent and bracket toward what looked like a big patch of reeds. When a dog grabs a scent, they move back and forth in a pattern—bracketing—to narrow down the source of the scent. Little did I know that the patch of reeds actually fell off after about twenty feet into a larger runoff. The two guys had hunkered down into the reeds and didn't realize that Brando hunted them.

Almost immediately, Brando darted out of my sight. The overhead asset told me that the dog had engaged one guy while the other one began beating Brando. We quickly moved up to where the dog and the two combatants fought. The overhead asset told us that the bad guys had attempted to toss Brando over the edge of a twenty-foot drop-off. However, Brando stayed in the fight.

Normally, Brando would have continued to stay on the bite until we moved up, but we did things a little bit differently in those days and decided to call Brando off the bite. Then, we demanded for them to come out. The first one obeyed the interpreter's command. It happened to be the guy that Brando had bitten. The second guy didn't understand or was just stupid because he refused to emerge. He simply stayed put. So I sent Brando in for another bite. He stayed on the bad guy until we moved in, but we called him off since the guy didn't have any weapons. Brando did well that night.

On the way back, we had to go through the shit-filled water again. We found it even funnier that time since we were no longer chasing after somebody. That had to be the nastiest crap I had ever smelled. Nasty and smelly but a glorious feeling knowing that Brando had found the bad guys and we had completed our mission.

As rapper Warren G would say, "It was a clear black night, a clear white moon." We would be going back out. So Brando and I strapped up for a crazy night. I looked forward to that mission because we would rope in on a mountain in a valley. We would surely have some work ahead of us. Maybe one bite, maybe more, but hey, I wanted to get after it with the crusaders of the squadron I rode with.

Brando got amped once I put his vest on—I only put it on for training or the real deal. I mainly did that for consistency. I wanted something to trigger in the dog's brain that putting on his vest meant time for work.

Constant repetition with an animal is the easiest way to teach them what you want to teach them. Want to have a chaotic animal? Be inconsistent and leave them always wondering what will happen next. That's extremely unfair for the dog, so I always made sure I went through the same routine, over and over.

I checked Brando's equipment and went over my own gear, making sure that I had everything I needed. That included verifying that I'd loaded the route into my GPS and that all of my IR lights worked. It's super important to turn on those IR strobes while chasing squirters. It tells everyone else wearing night vision, or even the assets in the sky, who you are.

I packed my Coca-Cola plus water for the dog. Geared up and ready, Brando and I sat in the team room. Everyone went through their tasks, and then came my turn. I said I'd be ready to send it whenever needed. I was always ready to send the dog when called up. If someone hid, I always had confidence we'd find them. I would roll in with Alpha Team after we roped in off the helicopter.

I muzzled Brando up, and we boarded the helicopters. Once on board, I positioned myself toward the back so I could go out first to the right rear of the helicopter while the rest of the team started to go out the left. Brando sat quietly through the ride, though he yawned. He wasn't tired; yawning signifies stress in a dog. I experienced a little stress as well on occasion. As a non-SEAL, I had constant pressure to perform.

When we reached about ninety seconds out, I started to make my way to the ramp behind our EOD tech. Usually, they would hold onto us while we clipped in the device. My kit had a little handle on the back that he could hold—a critical step because, at any time, the helicopter could shift abruptly, and I had no interest in getting pitched out the back of that thing. The EOD tech grabbed the dog by the vest and grabbed me by the back of my plate carrier. I took the Y-shaped carabiner hooked to the dog and myself and attached it to the device.

Thirty seconds came over the radio. Game time. A fast rope to the ground. *It's happening*, I thought.

Just like OTBs, that turned my stomach to knots. I had confidence in how to fast rope but always found it nerve-racking on a real mission. We needed to get down that rope as fast as possible, unclip from the device, and then hold security while everyone else came down.

The ramp tech gave the signal to go. I pulled the safety pin, grabbed Brando, and swung out. The dog really didn't know the real thing versus training. I'm sure he could feel my adrenaline, but the dog had no choice but to swing out with me, and down the rope we went. Just like that, we reached the bottom, and I pulled the device down to the ground so that the boys wouldn't hit it.

My heart beat fast as I held security while everyone else came down. Brando lay there on the ground in a down position just like we trained every time. Out the left side of the helicopter, the team came down as well, so when I hit the ground, I wasn't alone. I thought that stuff was fun.

Brando and I would go with RECCE to lead the way down a really shitty walk. You would think walking down a mountain would be easier than walking up, but I found the opposite to be true. About five minutes into the patrol, I found a big stick that looked like it was made for a walking stick. Literally too good to be true. That stick came in handy.

After an uneventful walk toward our objective, we reached our first building, and the team started to go silent. We kept the dog back to keep things stealthy. After the first house, however, we shifted to calling people out of the buildings. In the second building, we noticed a freaking DShK machine gun. I'm forever grateful that no one had manned it while we walked down the side of the mountain.

Soon, we heard that squirters had run a bit away from us, and we'd have to deal with them. As we moved through, the team started to become thin. There were many small buildings, and we kept finding noncombatants that needed watching. I continued sending Brando and following my team leader.

At some point, the team leader and I approached this one building. We heard over comms that overhead assets had engaged the one squirter who had some type of weapon.

The team leader looked back at me. "Is this all we got?" Meaning just him and me. Then, he asked, "You good?"

"I'm good if you're good," I replied.

"Let's send the dog."

My main job was to work the dog. I didn't specialize in clearing houses, but if needed, I was capable. I was fortunate that the guy trusted me to do that with him. We sent Brando, and he found nothing. We cleared the house, which consisted of several rooms, with no incident.

Time to deal with the squirter. Nothing like hunting someone down. I don't really know how to describe the exhilaration, but I imagine that's what cocaine or any other addictive drug feels like. The squirter ducked behind rocks after we engaged him. At that point, we weren't sure whether he was dead or not, so like with any other squirter, we pushed up to the area. The terrain always amazed me. Gigantic rocks surrounded us. It was a truly beautiful place. It's too bad you can't just go and hike in Afghanistan.

I sent Brando out multiple times, and he kept searching. As we moved through the rocks, he caught the scent and took off. We patrolled up and found him chewing on the guy. He had to have crawled to where he lay motionless. The guy had an AK-47 in his hand, but we didn't know his status: dead or alive. As Brando engaged him, we placed some careful shots, then continued searching but found no one else. As we walked out, jumping down terrace to terrace to the exfil site, I popped open my Coke and enjoyed the walk, my gun in one hand and my Coke in the other.

Brando and I also went on another mission with the Army Rangers that deployment. I found the Rangers to be some good dudes, and had I never worked with the SEAL teams, I would have switched branches to try to make it through their selection. Every time I went out with them, I knew that I'd experience the same professionalism that I experienced with my SEAL buddies. Sure, most considered the Rangers to be a step below the SEAL Team ██ guys, but they were good. People get caught up in that "which unit is better" BS. We were all there to do the same thing. They had one major difference in the way they worked the dog. So I always had a goal to show them a better way. I usually got pushy and would jump further up the stack. I sure as hell used that to my full advantage.

On one particular operation, it got kind of squirrely. Brando had worked as a sport dog candidate before we got him. One of those exercises involved a bark and hold behind a blind. That could prove troublesome, especially when we were out on an operation and someone was hiding. In training, we teach all the dogs to bite people who are not moving in case they are playing possum or if they are hiding and can be taken down by the dog. On the other hand, the bark and hold in sport work is where the dog goes up to the decoy and just barks. I'm dumbing it down a lot, but that's basically what happens. If a dog does that on target, there's a chance they will be dead because it allows the bad guy to grab a gun. We want them eating as soon as they find someone.

One night when we patrolled in, it was more or less like any other walk-in except the Rangers decided to land further out, and we really had to hike in. I would normally let Brando range out in front, but these weren't my guys, so I decided to just keep him on leash. Like I'd seen before, those Rangers humped in all this equipment, and one even carried a ladder. That dude was smoked by the time we got to the target, but he did it. Eight kilometers to the target, and he carried all that crap.

We reached the building, and because we tried to win the hearts and minds, we asked people inside to come out so that no one would get hurt. Meanwhile, three squirters had hunkered down, but we kept watch ██████ ██████. They weren't moving, so we decided to take down the initial target buildings. After the callout, I sent Brando into the courtyard and let him work. Originally, the Rangers planned to make entry first, but I requested over the radio for us to let the dog do his thing first. They let him, and I'm thankful they did.

It reached a point where only me, Brando, and another Ranger stood at one particular target location. While Brando searched, we saw something moving underneath a nearby stack of blankets. Brando began barking, and I told the Ranger that we had something. The blankets were large enough to cover a grown adult, so we could guess what was causing them to move. However, at that point, we didn't know what was under there and certainly wouldn't shoot until we did. It could be a kid or a Taliban fighter with explosives. We routinely risked our lives versus doing something stupid that could wind up putting us in jail. I'd seen that situation before with Breston in an earlier deployment.

I covered the pile with my gun while the Ranger began removing blankets. It ended up being a cradle three feet off the ground with a baby in it. I was so pissed that the adults in the building hadn't taken the baby with them. Thankfully, Brando hadn't worked harder on that particular target. As I mentioned before, dogs don't distinguish from man, woman, child, or baby. They will bite whatever is there for the taking. As sad as that sounds, it's something that I've experienced before. I've had dogs bite women and kids. It is neither pretty nor perfect. You can't put it in a box and expect it to stay in that box. To muddle things even further, I've had women and kids come out fully armed, so we had to be ready for anything, and so did the dogs. But luckily, in this instance, the baby remained safe.

We had several squirters that remained hunkered down, and we needed to catch them. So we sent Brando out after the squirters while we followed behind. Brando kept bracketing in the trees, back and forth. I could tell Brando had picked up on an odor, as he kept throwing his head up and back and forth, bracketing faster and faster in the trees. I stood in the middle of a wedge that we'd formed, and I could hear Brando barking. Typically, our dogs would bark when they found someone who was inaccessible, so I assumed that was the case here. However, as we worked our way up to Brando, I could see the guy was just standing next to the tree while Brando sat there, barking and keeping guard on him. I found it hard to watch because I knew that the sport work had come out in that scenario.

We had to improvise. That guy wouldn't show his hands as commanded by the interpreter, so I told Brando to *stellen,* at which point he grabbed the guy by his arm and pulled him to the ground. At ninety pounds, a Dutch shepherd with Brando's size and intensity can pretty much take anyone down. I praised Brando from afar, telling him "good boy" and "*stellen.*" I called Brando off, and after that, the guy did everything we requested of him. I was perfectly in my right to let Brando deal with him. If we would have killed him for being non-compliant, the people who make all the decisions would have had our asses. To this day, I'm happy with how it turned out.

Chapter 14
PATRIOT DOG

A much-needed and anticipated homecoming from that deployment came in October of 2011. We had lost so many of our brothers and friends on that deployment. I don't believe we had yet gotten a chance to mourn their loss because we had continued doing what we did best—taking the fight to the enemy. If drinking through our loss filled the need for some of that mourning, then we certainly did our best with that. I don't know what seemed worse: staying back and continuing the fight while the U.S. Navy flew the boys back to their final resting places or flying back with them and attending all the funerals. I think at the time I became numb to all of it, and going out on missions occupied my mind.

Because I stayed after Extortion 17, it meant that the time had eventually come to go home and face reality. I had to experience that homecoming without so many people that should have come home with us. I think I could say for the first time in my life I felt happy knowing that I'd likely no longer deploy with SEAL Team ██. Extortion 17 was not only a huge loss for me, but my family had become so close to Jet. That event made the decision for me. I knew right then and there I would not be coming back.

My wife picked me up in our SUV, and my daughter, not yet three, practically fell out of the window trying to get to me. My son had barely reached four years old.

I didn't know if my time in the navy would end just yet. I took about a month's leave so that I could spend time with my family and decompress from the past four months—really, four years. The holidays approached, so we took a vacation, which allowed me to live a little more in reality. I remember driving down the streets in the middle of the night a couple of times and looking at how different everything was. I had become so used to everything overseas and the way of life for people over there. I had forgotten that no matter how bad I had it, a day in my life was likely better than a lifetime of living over there for most people.

In July 2012, I completed the necessary steps and drove out of the gate at SEAL Team ▮, leaving the command and kennel behind. I would miss the boys (and women) that I had served with, but to hell with the rest of it. Especially the politics that put our lives in danger overseas. I felt a huge weight lifted off of me.

I needed a fresh start and chose JEB Little Creek. Many navy families live in the Virginia Beach area. The entire region is filled with both historic and military locations, such as the Jamestown settlement; Colonial Williamsburg; Newport News Shipbuilding, where aircraft carriers are built; Naval Station Norfolk, the largest naval base in the world; Naval Air Station Oceana; and ▮▮▮▮ JEB Little Creek sat in the middle of all that.

At the time, I thought that leaving would solve all my problems, but that couldn't have been further from the truth. I would soon face the harsh reality of moving from a fast-paced operational tempo to a much more relaxed one. I would be going to Little Creek to essentially sit at a desk and run the kennel as the kennel master. I had not thought through how that would impact me. Although I knew that I needed a break, I didn't realize that it would affect me the way it did.

When I left SEAL Team ▮, I was a wreck. I wanted to finish out my twenty years so I could retire. I could somehow deal with my own issues from my injuries, but I could not process losing Jet, Bart, and the boys on Extortion 17. My mind hurt, and my body hurt even worse.

I somehow managed to make chief petty officer, a huge step for an enlisted sailor, because of my service record, but I was not in it to win it, as they say. I remained on edge so much that during my chief season (a time when all the newly selected chiefs prepare to put on their anchors), I messed up a little.

They'd occasionally check to see if any of us were overweight, and while we were standing in line, a command master chief of one of the participating commands, who I didn't know at the time, asked if the wristband I wore was authorized by the navy. That particular bracelet had the words Extortion 17 on it so I could remind myself daily of my purpose. It also happened to be the one-year anniversary of the incident, so I was more on edge than ever that day.

I looked at him, not realizing who he was, and said, "I don't know, but I'd like to see a motherfucker try to take it off."

Someone pulled me aside, explaining that I had been out of line. I owned that mistake, but it speaks to how on edge I remained. I would later meet with that master chief who offered me some good advice that I simply needed to get help. Honestly, his advice was the reason why I sought help with the things I was going through. He had been through the USS *Cole* attack and understood what I was experiencing.

I applied and the U.S. Navy selected me for limited duty officer (LDO), a goal I'd had since I joined. This meant that I'd become an officer working in a specific role, but an LDO doesn't rise in rank to command a ship or anything like that. I would have tried for an LDO specific role, such as security officer or something similar, had I continued on that path.

However, I just had nothing left in me. I started to see a psychiatrist and began talking to someone about my migraines and issues with my legs. I would literally sit in my office and cry for no reason. I had a strange period where I remained strong at times but, for some reason, would crumble. I would drive to the base and pull over because I couldn't help but just cry.

Anytime helicopters flew over the base, I thought about my time overseas and felt the desire to go back there. To numb my mind, I would take Vicodin and drink a couple of beers. I began my routine on Friday and found ways to justify doing it Saturday as well. Eventually, it became a daily habit. I got to where I looked forward to that to help with pain and take away my sadness.

I honestly can't believe I'm admitting that. I think the reason why I decided to open up about everything from being molested to growing up without a father to my struggles with losing friends is because it seemed selfish for me not to share.

I do believe you truly can overcome anything in life. I mean that and say that with all the conviction in me because I've seen a lot and experienced a lot. Is it easy? No, definitely not. It requires a lot of self-determination to want to get better and to do better. You have to do it for yourself. There's nothing wrong with admitting that something is too much to bear and moving on to something else. During that last deployment, knowing it would be my last because of Extortion 17, I had decided to give it everything I had and then call it done. I loved my job, but the psychological impact had become too much. Our minds are powerful, but at the same time, we have to remember that everyone has a point at which they can't take it anymore, and a change needs to happen. Look at anything in your life that's not working and consider making a change.

It's never too late to make a change, but prepare yourself for the fact that it may not be what you wanted. I left SEAL Team ▌, something only a few people get to experience, and returned to the big navy only to find out that even that wasn't enough. I realized that I had lost my love for the navy and the mental impact of my experiences weighed on me too much. At some point, I had to own up to it and say, "You know what, it's okay to pivot. Not quit but pivot."

Even with help from professionals, I still found myself crying in my car while headed to work and thinking it's not worth it. Was it worth me contemplating taking my own life just to make it end? No, it wasn't, and luckily for me, I knew I had Jesus in my heart, and I knew that suicide would not get me any closer to Him. I also had a family to think of, so that gave me enough to live for.

As a chief, and possibly soon an officer, I struggled with my lack of drive for the navy. I kept fighting it because I was doing what I thought everyone else wanted me to do. I had all the awards and ribbons for an MA. I had a really great career.

I once had an event on the USS *Constitution* (a museum ship) where they brought in a bunch of chief petty officer selectees for a week. On the last day, we wore our dress blues that included all of our ribbons and other shiny things that we wear on our uniform. Naturally, I was proud of what I had accomplished and wore those on my uniform. I had a couple of good friends there who knew what I had been through. They heard a few people talking about that MA who had a purple heart and how I probably had practiced stolen valor. I just laughed because who in their right mind would put on fake ribbons or medals at that type of event? That event added to a list of many other reasons, but the time for a change had come.

I made it to January 2013, eighteen months after Extortion 17. After several talks with my doctors and the surgeon who saw my aftercare, I decided that my situation warranted a medical board to consider medically retiring me. My legs and migraines had not improved, and my PTSD was becoming debilitating. I had stayed in that dark place for too long with no hope of moving past it. I constantly relived the event, the loss, and the pain. The time had come. My chain of command supported me. My chief's mess (the other chiefs close to me) also took care of me when I couldn't due to my appointments. I had a family to think about, and I really didn't have plans for after the navy, but I knew we'd be okay.

Extortion 17 continued to weigh on me mentally. I don't think a day went by that I did not think about all of those guys. On top of that, I struggled with my physical health. I had lied to myself for so many years, saying that I was fine and that nothing bothered me. Deep down inside, I knew that my legs hurt. I think it's safe to say that I had the lasting effects of chronic pain from the building IED in 2008. My hips hurt the most—they still do. It's not easy to describe, but it sort of feels like two rocks grinding together when I walk. On top of that, the soreness can linger throughout the day.

I'm not one to simply complain and tried to hide it because, after all, I still had my legs while so many others lost theirs from their injuries. To be honest, the amount of pain for all those years did not outweigh the joy I had going out on ops with the boys. Similarly, I now explain that to owners about their dogs. Dogs will go through an enormous amount of discomfort if the reward or drive for the reward outweighs the pain they're feeling. The opposite can occur as well. Sometimes, the discomfort will be too much to consider doing the behavior.

The medical board went smoothly for me. I've heard from so many that it does not always go that way. I wasn't one to look for an easy way out. But I do believe they saw my medical record with all the documented surgeries and brain studies and probably thought *that dude is screwed* and signed off. Kidding, of course. I'm sure they conducted a much more in-depth review.

In the end, they approved me for a medical discharge, which left me with the U.S. Department of Veterans Affairs (VA). This presented a whole other animal. While searching the web for how the VA's process worked, it amazed me how many out there were just trying to cheat the system and grab that 100 percent. I had no intention of cheating on anything. I went through all my exams with the doctors and psychologists, and they determined me 100 percent disabled.

I hate that term by the way—disabled. It makes us veterans appear as though we are weak.

When I sat down with the psychologist and told her my experiences, I shared about Extortion 17. I described having to go through the gear and everything that wasn't human remains from that helicopter in the days after and how the smell of burnt flesh stuck with me. By the end of those sessions, I'm not sure how she didn't seek help for herself after having to listen to the things I told her. I remember during the psych exam, I sat and told the psychologist all of my shit, and by the end of it, she just had this blank stare.

I was only rated 10 percent for each leg, which came as a huge surprise to me. The VA uses an elaborate manual and special math for those percentage determinations. Apparently, pain doesn't factor as much compared to something like range of motion. So while I had debilitating pain, I had really outdone myself during my initial recovery to achieve stellar range of motion.

I officially retired from the U.S. Navy on October 29, 2013, two years after my return from Afghanistan. Honestly, I felt like a quitter but was no longer trapped in the cage that my mind had locked me in. I drove off the base for the last time that day and only returned once for the memorial of a sailor who sadly committed suicide. I really wish he would have asked for help. He left a lot of people sad and wondering why.

Although I had been made a chief petty officer and been selected for LDO, huge accomplishments for me, I remained unhappy. At that point, no promotion or amount of money could feed me mentally. Was it a financial risk to step away? Yes, of course. The navy paid for our housing, basic pay (salary), all medical expenses, etc., but none of it seemed worth it.

I suspected then and know with confidence now that when you look at kids as they grow and mature, they do need all their studies in various fields, but they also know to follow their deepest passion. I know that sounds kind of cliché, but think about it for a moment. Would you rather do something you hate for the rest of your life or pursue things that you enjoy? You can absolutely make a living doing the things you enjoy in life. How many people look back on their life and wish they would have chosen a different career?

I experienced an odd few months after retirement. I felt like a great weight had lifted off of my shoulders once I left the navy. I had earned a bachelor's degree in criminal justice during my time in the navy, even taking classes while on deployment. There were times when I returned from an operation killing and biting people with my dog to go have discussions in class not a couple hours later on just random shit.

However, I knew that I didn't want to pursue that field any further. So I applied everywhere and for everything, but companies passed on me for so many jobs. They found me either overqualified or underqualified. I literally applied to places like The Home Depot and Walmart, and they told me, "Thanks, but no thanks." I couldn't even get an interview. I applied for over thirty jobs on USAJOBs and received a fat zero for interviews. I'm not dogging any of the places that didn't hire me, but once again, I found myself in the gutter. It became a blessing in disguise, however, because I had worked for a paycheck for my whole life with the mindset to match. It pushed me toward the path of entrepreneurship.

It began one day when a neighbor asked if I could help with their dog. They knew I had worked as a dog handler and trainer. I gladly said yes. They had issues with the dog jumping and doing things that all disobedient dogs love to do. I went to their house, helped them work through a few things, and it all went well. They paid me for the work, and that's when it clicked in my head. I could actually make money training dogs for people. I had spent so much time trying to work for someone else when I could actually work for myself.

I then told Erica that I wanted to go to a training school to learn more about methods and best practices. As crazy as it sounded, Erica supported me. I applied to the Tom Rose School, run by an expert in the field of dog training. I had so much experience, but I always had a rule that I would never stop learning, no matter how good I became at something. I attended the school and never looked back. I knew that I had found what I was truly meant to do at that stage in my life.

In order to get the VA to use my benefits for the Tom Rose School, I had to jump through some hoops. Some VA counselors didn't understand that I could make it training dogs. I can't blame them though. In 2015, at an Inc. 5000 conference, a couple of people mocked me, saying, "There's no way you can make a living training dogs." An underdog yet again. Most people can only see what is right in front of them, and that's okay. I wasn't willing to take no for an answer.

While at the school in Missouri, I called Erica and asked her if she wanted to stay in Virginia Beach. I knew I could never "move on" while living there because my former command seemed like a cloud over me. It didn't feel like home anyway. We both agreed to move, so she packed up the house, and we went to Illinois to live with my in-laws until we could figure out where we wanted to land.

I graduated from the Tom Rose School as one of the top students in my class. My experience and training in the military had never included raising a pup, teaching it the basics, and then moving on to more advanced skills, but I learned all of that during the program. That would become extremely helpful since I would deal with new pet parents as part of my business. I met a lot of people during that course and loved to see young kids right out of high school all the way up to people in their fifties and sixties. It only proved to me that you don't necessarily need a college degree for everything to find success.

I joined Erica and the kids in Chicago to live with my in-laws for almost a year. Most people would hate living with their in-laws, but mine were really different and such amazing people. It was almost the perfect scenario for our family at the time because our kids could spend time with their grandparents, and we had the chance to look at where we actually wanted to live.

I started off on rover.com, just boarding some dogs. Did I already mention that my in-laws were awesome? At one point, I had a few dogs in one of their bedrooms and then dogs in their basement. More than a few actually. I had roughly twenty dogs at one point in their home. We kept it really clean and could manage a few dogs at a time while also training a few dogs as well.

I knew I wasn't going to stay in Chicago, so I didn't want to go all out, although I could have because the internet made it possible for anyone to find me and hire me for that work. Finally, in 2015, we decided to move to Boerne, Texas, just outside of San Antonio. After attending a veterans entrepreneurship program at the University of Florida, I met a presenter who came from Boerne. Erica and I flew down there to take a look. We absolutely loved the area and decided to have a house built for our family.

Most people would cringe at the idea of moving to some random area in the United States where they had never lived, not only to start a new life but to open a new business with no promise of success. I had grown up with a family that worked blue-collar jobs but left that mentality behind me and would no longer chase a paycheck. I decided to completely and exclusively answer to God. I had Erica by my side, and she remained more than supportive. We knew we'd face challenges, but I kept the "why" always there. I did it for my family, not for money. The money would come as a byproduct of that success for staying focused on the why.

We had built a brand-new house on five acres. I put several crates in my two-car garage and began to advertise in the area about my new business. We lived twenty minutes away from San Antonio, Texas, so I really had to focus on local businesses to get the word out. Veterinarian clinics, other kennels, and pet stores became huge promoters.

I grew fast, and people who had their dogs trained with me soon wanted boarding. They didn't want their freshly trained dog boarded at a place where the same skills and rules that I taught wouldn't be at the forefront. I then decided to build a small eight-dog kennel with about 1,200 square feet of training space. I thought that would serve our needs, but once again, I was wrong. I would outgrow that in such a short amount of time that I would soon have to look for space outside of my property. I eventually found four thousand square feet of space out in town. I put twenty-six kennels there and quickly realized again that I had gone too small. Not a bad problem to have, but at some point, you just have to say *enough*. We decided to stop at ten thousand square feet with just over seventy spaces for the dogs.

I found it challenging to hire people who could train at the level I required and discovered that it watered down our product and service. I simply would never let quality suffer. Eventually, after learning how to find the right people, I *did* find the right people. To this day, Patriot Dog Training offers training to pet owners all over the United States. I've had so many people ask me to train their dogs, from the person next door to professional athletes. I've even driven the Sprinter van in the dead of winter to Minnesota to pick up ten dogs and bring them down to Texas for training. I've picked up dogs in Los Angeles and returned them all trained to their owners. On some occasions, we have even procured several protection dogs for clients. For the most part, helping dog owners connect with their animals has provided a most rewarding experience. Like any other business, we certainly get our share of difficult customers, but the good far outweighs the bad.

Entrepreneurship is often about taking chances. I thought that I needed to simply go get a job and work for someone. Society programs us to think that way. Schools play a big role in teaching our kids that. I worked for the navy for ten years, and for ten years, I received a regular paycheck. That provided comfort, except it programmed me with too much reliance on it. That gave me the attitude that I simply needed to go for reliability. For comfort.

The more I thought about it though, I came to realize I wanted something more. I wanted to take another chance on myself. I am glad every single day that I opted for the unknown. It became another case of me facing a long line of doubters. The ones calling me an underdog. The ones who cautioned me to do something safer. I aimed for what felt right to me.

Those last couple of years in the navy, I had lost my will to send it. My passion had disappeared. I had no greater thrill in life than standing on target with my dog. Him pulling the leash taut. Salivating to go get the bad guy. Me holding the leash and waiting for the command to send the dog. I was always ready to send it, and I'm thrilled with Patriot Dog Training as we continue to send it to this day.

———————

While my story continues as I navigate life, I'm sure many readers may be curious about the dogs I served with. Most went on to retire with their handlers. I always had a cherished place in my heart for Digo, but it simply wasn't practical to have him come live at my home with children. Digo, while sweet at times, remained sort of a loose cannon with a few quirks.

Former Navy SEAL Mike Ritland, who created the Warrior Dog Foundation, took Digo. From their mission statement, the foundation "transitions our country's working K9s from an operational environment into retirement. Providing mental and physical rehabilitation, and rehoming options to Military Working Dogs (MWD), Contract Working Dogs (CWD), and Law Enforcement K9s that otherwise would be euthanized." Mike created a great location for them on his ranch that offers a fine retirement to those heroes.

Digo would eventually live on the ranch until he was adopted by someone who could provide him with the exact things he needed to find success in a home environment. Digo died a few years later on a couch in Florida with his favorite toy. It brought me happiness knowing that he lived out his days comfortably on a couch.

Breston was never really my dog. They had "lent" him to me for deployment, but I definitely could see the similarities between him and Digo. Like Digo, he went to the Warrior Dog Foundation for the remainder of his life.

The only dog that I could absolutely have around my kids was Brando, but he retired and lived out his days with a SEAL from the command. At first, that made me salty. I felt like they had denied me Brando because I had started writing this book and also because I wasn't a SEAL. However, he ended up with a SEAL I'm very fond of, so in the end, it didn't matter. I think it was Brando who provided me comfort during my last deployment and ultimately kept me alive. My family was reason enough, but when they weren't there, he was.

I'm thankful for the work of the Warrior Dog Foundation and many others that provide these amazing animals with the life they deserve after their service to our great nation. It's a great example of appreciation for those who served just as I've benefited from organizations that appreciated my service. Some of us who went on target have survivor's guilt. We struggled with coming home when some of our friends didn't. I draw peace from knowing that I gave the best I had to offer—that I sent it.

Afterword by
ANONYMOUS

W e served with Benito Olson. Some of us wore Tridents as Navy SEALs, and some didn't. Some of us served on the SEAL teams, and some of us did not. However, all had the privilege to work with one of the finest military dog handlers in the United States arsenal. During NFL quarterback Troy Aikman's Hall of Fame enshrinement speech, he offered an interesting thank-you to his long-time fullback, a position during their era that mainly provided blocking duties. Not the most glamorous role. He said, "Daryl 'Moose' Johnston, the blue-collar guy who I'm not ashamed to say was better at his job than any other player on the team was theirs, including myself." Benito, or Benny as we called him, was that blue-collar guy that showed up every day, worked to become the best at his "position," and always had our back. We all swore an allegiance to defend our country to the best of our abilities, even if that meant the last full measure of devotion.

Benny makes an interesting first impression, especially for someone desiring to work with the SEAL teams. At first, he seemed too small. Could he keep up with our long hikes and tall climbs, with the carrying of heavy loads and the carrying of a dog, and with the operational tempo unseen in most other units? He looked so young. Would he have the maturity and experience to match the mission we had? Would he have the ability to make life-and-death decisions in an instant? He seemed so quiet. Did he remain that way over fear or uncertainty? Many of us considered him to be an underdog as a support person for the SEAL teams.

We soon realized that he had the physical tools to keep up with us and get the job done with a work ethic off the charts. We found out that despite his age, he showed the maturity to match what we needed for our missions. He caught on quickly, and we didn't have to worry about him. Team members can function as an asset or a burden, and Benny with his dog proved to be a valuable asset. Yes, Benny remains a quiet guy. That's because of his humility. He truly functioned with the mindset that he didn't want to let any of us down. You won't hear him boasting about his exploits. However, we don't mind doing that.

Benny, like most of us, conducted so many missions through Iraq and Afghanistan that we cannot remember them all. Time in and time out, he had his dog ready. Dogs that became legends in themselves such as Digo, Breston, and Brando. When we called on him to send the dog, he never hesitated and, many times, exposed himself to great harm in doing so by moving across open terrain where bullets flew. On that fateful day in Iraq when the enemy blew up a house with an IED, we saw his injuries and thought he'd never return to the battlefield. We didn't think a Team Guy (SEAL team member) would have returned from that. Yet Benny fought through his underdog status and did return. We couldn't believe it. He not only returned, but he also hadn't slowed down a bit from his previous abilities. If anything, he felt the need to prove himself all over again with new dogs.

We had one mission that required a lot of climbing, up and down, on steep terrain. Simply exhausting. Benny not only made the climb, but he did it with legs that had rods holding together his femurs, and he also had to carry the dog at times. Sometimes, the trek to the battlefield presented the most daunting task of a particular mission. During most of the missions, the dog handler and dog stayed near the front but were not necessarily "kicking down the door." On one particular mission, due to the number of targets, we became somewhat separated, so Benny, without hesitation, took the lead spot and kicked down the door. He never hesitated to provide effective suppressing fire to cover us. He truly had our backs.

The term "Band of Brothers" has become almost cliché, but that doesn't make it any less true. It's evidenced by the way we talk about Benny and the way he refers to us but even more so by how we speak of our brothers we've lost. Those like Mike Koch, Nate Hardy, Luis Souffront, and all those on that tragic day when Extortion 17 went down. We were and are brothers. We're proud to have served with Benny and call him our brother.

Benny often says, "I wasn't a SEAL." It's funny how people will bring that up when learning he served with a SEAL team. As if they need to remind him. He's never claimed it. It's almost as if they feel the need to accuse him of stolen valor. In our view, he epitomizes valor. When you're watching a ball game, sitting around the table at Thanksgiving, witnessing the birth of your child, or enjoying any number of other freedoms, you have people like Benito Olson to thank. Him and his incredible dogs.

ACKNOWLEDGMENTS

There are so many people to thank for the completion of this book and my life, but if there's one thing that's true, it's that I couldn't have done this without GOD and my belief in Jesus. If GOD is with you, then certainly NOTHING can be against you.

There are so many people who've been a big deal in my life. And this time around, I really have to give a shoutout to my amazing wife, Erica. I've said it before, and I'll say it again: you've been by my side through thick and thin. You stuck around when you didn't have to, and man, you sure didn't bail out even when I was acting like a total mess. It's pretty clear to me that someone upstairs had a hand in this crazy journey. Take my boot camp graduation, for example. You weren't even in my life back then, but lo and behold, thanks to God's intervention, your cousin ended up in the same division as me. Go figure, right? Looking back, that's some next-level coincidence. I can't help but feel so lucky to have you with me.

Now, onto my mom. There's not much else to say except you're a total badass. You busted your butt for us kids and showered us with so much love. Honestly, I owe my success to you—I wouldn't be here without your determination to make our lives better. Mom, I love you!

Dad, I gotta talk to you too. I know you've had your regrets about not being around when we were growing up. But seriously, I want you to know that you made me tough. I never held any of that against you, and honestly, being a dad ain't a walk in the park. We say it—you were just a kid having a kid. Love you, Dad.

Now, my children, I'm saving you for last. If there's one thing I've always wished for, it's to write this book for you so that, one day, you can read it to your own children once they are old enough. While I'm here putting this down, I can practically hear my daughter saying, "Hey, Dad, you didn't write enough about me!" Well, you've got a point. Those years are kind of a blur, mostly filled with deployments and that kind of stuff. But trust me, every moment with you brings a smile to my face. Jacob, you're my little man—always will be even though you are taller than me now. You've got such a big heart, and I'm beyond proud of the young man you're becoming. And my little Memmas (Emma)—yeah, I know that's gonna get an eyeroll from you—thanks for being the energy boost our family needed. You're like our Nala, the German shepherd I brought home for your mom before I deployed after you were born. You guys are lifesavers.

To everyone I've crossed paths with, I just want to say a huge thanks for having faith in me. And for those I haven't met who are reading this: fuck the haters and just go all in on life. No excuses—just send it.